TRADE IN TRANSITION

Exports from the Third World, 1840–1900

STUDIES IN SOCIAL DISCONTINUITY

Under the Consulting Editorship of:

CHARLES TILLY
University of Michigan

EDWARD SHORTER
University of Toronto

The list of titles in this series continues on the last page of this volume

TRADE IN TRANSITION
Exports from the Third World, 1840–1900

John R. Hanson II

Department of Economics
Texas A&M University
College Station, Texas

ACADEMIC PRESS

A Subsidiary of Harcourt Brace Jovanovich, Publishers

New York   London   Toronto   Sydney   San Francisco

ACADEMIC PRESS, INC.
111 Fifth Avenue, New York, New York 10003

United Kingdom Edition published by
ACADEMIC PRESS, INC. (LONDON) LTD.
24/28 Oval Road, London NW1 7DX

Library of Congress Cataloging in Publication Data

Hanson, John R
    Trade in transition.

    (Studies in social discontinuity)
    Bibliography: p.
    Includes index.
    1. Underdeveloped areas--Commerce--History.
I. Title. II. Series.
HF1413.H32   382'.6'091724   79-6776
ISBN 0-12-323450-6

PRINTED IN THE UNITED STATES OF AMERICA

80 81 82 83   9 8 7 6 5 4 3 2 1

To my parents

Contents

4
Destinations of Less Developed Countries' Exports in the Victorian Era

5
Determinants of Less Developed Countries' Exports, 1820–1860

6
Determinants of Less Developed Countries' Exports, 1860–1900

7
Tariffs, Transportation Costs, Exchange Rates, Terms of Trade, and Export Surpluses

Preface

The historical relationship between the less developed countries and the world economy has attracted significant academic and public attention in recent years, with the result that the number of books and articles on the subject has multiplied spectacularly. Yet empirical advances in the field have been few. In even the most comprehensive and scholarly treatments, old data are merely reinterpreted, often from a Marxist point of view, and little new information is contributed. The need for further historical–empirical research on the network of world trade has become increasingly apparent, however. We still do not know, for example, what were the main outlets for LDC products and how both products and outlets changed over time during the crucial nineteenth century. Accordingly, the purposes of this book are to fill part of the statistical gap concerning the place of the less developed countries in the network of world trade during the Victorian era and to show that the new data have major implications for existing ideas about the performance of the international capitalist economy since the Industrial Revolution. Capitalism has, of course, been under attack from many quarters in recent years.

Estimates of the composition of the exports of many of today's developing nations on both a commodity-by-commodity and region-by-region basis for several benchmark dates between 1840 and 1900 are the main statistical contribution of this book. In addition, new data concerning the magnitude of exports in relation to national or regional output in the developing nations during the Victorian era are presented and discussed. An original interpretation of these data is suggested which on many points conflicts with the conventional wisdom, especially that part of the conventional wisdom attributing monocausal significance to the rising demand for primary products in Western Europe as a determinant of the role to be occupied by the developing nations in the overall economic scheme.

Chapter 1 raises the main historical and analytical issues, which the data compiled here address, and introduces the main themes that are developed in subsequent chapters. Chapters 2, 3, and 4 summarize the main empirical findings. A tentative but provocative interpretation of the most important trends is presented in Chapters 5, 6, and 7. The key findings and conjectures are summarized in Chapter 8, where topics for further research are also suggested.

The book is directed at anyone interested in the history of economic relations between developed and developing countries. Nonetheless, professional economists and economic historians and their graduate students will most likely find the book of greatest interest because the ways in which the data might be used and the novelty of the analysis will be more apparent to them than to the layman. Still, an effort has been made to make the style and presentation as unforbidding as possible while not sacrificing adherence to accepted canons of scholarship.

I owe a debt of gratitude to everyone who helped in the preparation of this volume, but only a few can be mentioned. My parents provided more than just moral support. Richard Easterlin, friend and advisor since graduate school days, contributed sound advice as I pursued this intellectual exploration. My friends and colleagues at Texas A&M University, especially John Kagel and Raymond Battalio, also have been most helpful, and the Department of Economics provided a fertile environment for nurturing the ideas advanced here. Thomas Skidmore and Jeffrey Williamson offered suggestions and encouragement. Several secretaries contributed to making the original manuscript presentable, but the labors of Nancy Estes and Yvonne Evans are especially appreciated.

Appreciation is also expressed to the following publishers who gave me permission to use material in articles of mine originally published by them: Academic Press ("Diversification and Concentration of LDC Exports," *Explorations in Economic History* 14 [1977]: 44–68); The University of Chicago Press ("The Leff Conjecture: Some Contrary Evidence," *Journal of Political Economy* 84 [April 1976]: 401–405); and Cambridge University Press ("More on Trade as a Handmaiden of Growth," *Economic Journal* 87 [September 1977]: 554–557).

TRADE IN TRANSITION

Exports from the Third World, 1840–1900

1
Introduction

Focus of the Study

A massive and probably unprecedented expansion of the world economy accompanied the decline of the mercantilist empires and the international diffusion of industrialism during the nineteenth century. All parts of the globe were affected directly or indirectly, and it is generally believed that the foundations of the modern network of world trade were laid in the 100 years or so preceding World War I. Yet, as we shall see, orthodox economic historians have not provided a satisfactory account of either the part played by the less developed countries (LDCs) in this process or the effects of this process on the LDCs. Since exports from what is today called the Third World represented roughly 20% of world trade during the nineteenth century, the oversight is neither trivial from the academic viewpoint nor without consequence for the making of foreign policy by both developed and less developed nations in the modern world. Many of the issues in the strained and occasionally acrimonious "dialogue" that is being conducted between developed and less developed countries arise, after all, from conceptions about the functioning of the international capitalist economy since the Industrial Revolution.

In contrast to orthodox scholarship, radical and Marxist scholarship, which blames capitalism and imperialism for many problems in the Third World, emphasizes and dramatizes the historical relationship between the less developed nations and the international economy.[1] Broadly speaking, the leftists hold that the advanced countries used their superior strength,

[1]H. Brookfield, *Interdependent Development* (London: Methuen & Co., 1975). This is a thorough survey of the literature but stresses leftist contributions.

influence, and sophistication to twist the conditions of international exchange in their favor, thus inhibiting, if not altogether blocking, material progress in most of Asia, Africa, and Latin America. This interpretation bids fair to become orthodoxy in the Third World, especially among political elites, and is gaining adherents in the capitalist West. As a matter of fact, the inordinate sympathy for LDCs that is exhibited by certain groups in the Western democracies has helped in the identification of a new syndrome, "white liberal guilt," that critics of the exploitation thesis liken to a mass neurosis.

One regrettable similarity among historians of all stripes is that all too often they support sweeping generalizations about the role of the LDCs in the network of trade with sketchy statistical evidence and beg the most basic empirical questions. When did the LDCs enter the network of world trade? Was entry simultaneous or sequential? What was the growth rate of LDC exports at different times? How large were fluctuations in the rate? How extensive was the diversification of the products the LDCs exported? What were the main outlets for LDC products? How did these change over time? Lacking answers to these and related questions, we can only speculate about the historical role of the LDCs in the world economy.

The main purpose of this study is to provide information that will shed light on questions such as these and hence on other issues of concern to both developed and less developed countries. Together with the data provided in Yates's book *Forty Years of Foreign Trade,* a respected statistical survey of LDC trade between 1913 and 1953, and in the excellent statistical compendia supplied by international agencies during both the interwar and postwar periods, the data provided here make available a quantitative record of LDC exports running from the formative period of the modern network of world trade up to the present.[2] This information, imperfections notwithstanding, will help provoke a reexamination of existing conceptions about the historical relationship between the LDCs and the world economy.

An important difference between this history and others is the viewpoint governing the collection and processing of the basic data. Although excellent studies of particular LDCs are available, the data they present necessarily reflect a national perspective, not a global conception. Furthermore, the purposes and methodologies of the authors differ from investigation to investigation, with the result that the data offered are sometimes idiosyncratically chosen. For these reasons alone it would be fruitless to prepare a statistical history of the trade of the laggards in the growth race that depends primarily on case studies.

General treatments, such as Woodruff's *The Impact of Western Man,* rely

[2] P. L. Yates, *Forty Years of Foreign Trade* (New York: Macmillan, 1959).

heavily on the trade returns of today's developed countries in describing the position of the LDCs in the world economy.[3] But generalizations about the LDCs are inherently suspect if based solely on data that were gathered and processed from the perspective of, and for the purposes of, more advanced trading partners. Nor would it help to take a census of the trade returns of all recipients of export flows from LDCs, since accounting practices differ among even the most sophisticated and measurement-conscious nations.

This study adopts the LDC point of view but presents comprehensive statistics tracing the behavior of LDC exports during the nineteenth century that are based on the records of the LDCs themselves. Combining the non-Western perspective of the typical case study with the breadth of more comprehensive treatments, this approach realizes the best of both worlds. The framework is also flexible enough to allow material from studies reflecting other approaches to be included at appropriate points. Unfortunately, accounting practices among LDCs traditionally have not been any more comparable with each other than have accounting practices among advanced nations; nor are trade returns from LDCs always complete or reliable. But these are not insurmountable problems. Moreover, the conceptual advantages of adopting the LDC viewpoint are not lessened merely because LDC trade returns sometimes fall short of the highest statistical standards. Many fresh, provocative, and significant questions about the economic history of both developed and less developed nations also occur when a non-Western schema is employed.

The plan of this book is as follows. The remainder of this chapter expands on some of the points made so far and explains what the main analytical issues are and how they will be approached. Chapters 2, 3, and 4 are largely quantitative and descriptive. They treat a wide variety of topics, including the commodity and geographic composition of LDC exports during the nineteenth century. Although these chapters are largely informational, they also lay the groundwork for the main descriptive and analytical conclusions of the book. Some uninitiated readers may find these technical chapters tedious at times and possibly confusing, but the larger issues are kept in sight, and the summaries of the main empirical points are written with reference to them. Chapters 5, 6, and 7 contain an interpretation of the trends described in the previous three chapters. Because so much ground is covered in the empirical chapters, the analysis cannot be completely thorough; still, a persuasive case can be made for taking a fresh look at how the LDCs stood with respect to the nineteenth-century international economy. The final chapter summarizes the main findings and arguments of the study and suggests topics for further research.

[3] W. Woodruff, *The Impact of Western Man* (New York: St. Martin's Press, 1971).

Review of Existing Literature

The conventional wisdom in this area has been shaped by case studies of particular LDCs, by commodity histories, and, above all, by general descriptions of the evolution of the international economy. Let us concentrate temporarily on the broadest accounts, examining more narrowly conceived treatments later. Three influential and time-honored syntheses are Ashworth's short textbook, Youngson's lengthy article for the *Cambridge Economic History*, and Cole and Deane's summary article for the *Cambridge Economic History*.[4] These scholars examine international trade as a whole and are representative in treating the LDCs as a tangential part of the world economy. But later investigations focusing directly on the experience of tropical LDCs are compatible with the older works and, indeed, appear to draw on them. Two of these efforts are the 1969 Wicksell Lectures by the Nobel Prize winning economist W. Arthur Lewis and a collection of term papers by Lewis's students that begins with a lengthy and thoughtful introduction by the professor.[5] Ashworth writes:

> The increased specialization which characterized economic activity... was closely connected with the greater interdependence of the nations, which became still more marked as a result of the rapid growth of population.... The expansion of incomes promoted by great advances in productive technique stimulated a demand for a more diversified range of goods, which could only be satisfied by calling on resources hitherto unused and widely dispersed throughout the world. Such resources, or the fruits of their productive use, were obtainable only by exchange or conquest. The former method was... easier and certainly the more usual. Naturally, therefore, a great expansion took place in international trade.[6]

Ashworth considers the second half of the nineteenth century to have been a more significant era for the international economy than the first half, adding:

---

[4]W. Ashworth, *A Short History of the International Economy Since 1850* (London: Longmans, 1952); W. A. Cole and P. Deane, "The Growth of National Incomes," in *The Cambridge Economic History of Europe*, ed. H. J. Habbakkuk and M. Postan, Vol. 6 (London: Cambridge University Press, 1966), pp. 1–59; A. J. Youngson, "The Opening Up of New Territories," *ibid.*, pp. 139–211.

[5]W. A. Lewis, *Aspects of Tropical Trade, 1883–1965*, The Wicksell Lectures (Stockholm: Almqvist & Wicksell, 1969); W. A. Lewis, ed. *Tropical Development, 1880–1913* (Evanston, Ill.: Northwestern University Press, 1970). See bibliography for other contributions by this author. Lewis's most recent work, by the way, is exempt from some of the criticisms of other writers made in the text. It is more quantitative, for example. Nonetheless, Lewis writes from the same intellectual tradition as the senior historians discussed in the text, and his original empirical contributions have been modest. Interpretation is widely regarded as Lewis's forte.

[6]Ashworth, *International Economy Since 1850*, p. 163.

The overwhelming proportion of . . . international trade before 1850 had been conducted through restricted channels in a relatively small area, and the greater part of . . . economic activity had been of only domestic concern.[7]

The attention to post-1850 developments in world and LDC trade is shared by Cole and Deane, who observe:

It was through the international economy that the benefits of technological revolution were communicated to countries that did not themselves industrialize to any considerable extent. . . . Primary producers who were in no way stimulated to industrialize gained . . . from an increased world demand for imports of food and industrial raw materials. . . . The half-century before the First World War was the period within which the international economy began its massive expansion.[8]

Youngson agrees:

The international trading relations of the second half of the 19th century . . . were of a considerably more intimate and much more complex nature than those which had preceded them. . . . The economic organization of a great number of countries thus became . . . dependent upon the system of organization which embraced them all. This was a novel situation.[9]

Ashworth, Cole and Deane, Youngson, and others contend that one of the main reasons for the revolution in world economic relations was rising income and population in Western Europe. Eurocentrism, in fact, is the hallmark of the literature in this field, but most treatments fail to distinguish among the various parts of Western Europe. The United Kingdom, for example, is combined with other countries in the region, although the impact on world trade of economic development in Great Britain, the most powerful economy on earth, may have been different from the impact of economic development elsewhere in Europe or, for that matter, elsewhere in the world. The importance of this matter can hardly be overstated, and it will occupy our attention in much of the remainder of this volume. Yet Ashworth, to cite one example, makes only a slight distinction:

Throughout the period 1850–1914, international trade was dominated by the great industrial countries, especially by the U.K. Naturally, as new areas of supply were opened as the most advanced productive techniques became more widely diffused, the dominance of these few countries tended to diminish somewhat, but it remained great.[10]

[7]*Ibid.*
[8]Cole and Deane, "Growth of National Incomes," p. 171.
[9]Youngson, "New Territories," p. 171.
[10]Ashworth, *International Economy Since 1850,* p. 166.

But perhaps the most serious criticism of the standard accounts is that their treatments are largely qualitative. The passages just quoted are representative in offering little quantitative evidence to support generalizations and in glossing over important empirical questions, such as those listed earlier in this chapter. Indeed, it is not unfair to say that the conventional wisdom about the pattern of evolution of the international economy has become self-reinforcing and that it is accepted to a degree not warranted by the thin descriptive statistical evidence that has so far been compiled on the relationship of the European "center" to the non-European "periphery." This is also true in Andre Gunder Frank's treatment of the alleged role of export surpluses in the underdevelopment of the Third World. This issue will be examined in Chapter 7.

Analytically, the main issue is whether or not the LDCs benefited from export-led economic development following their entrance into the world economy. Radicals and Marxists, of course, believe that they did not. Another scholar, Myint, opines that dynamic gains in the poor countries prior to World War I were modest at best.[11] Case studies of several Latin American countries by Leff (Brazil), Levin (Peru), and Mandle (British Guiana) support this conclusion.[12] Lewis, on the other hand, uses the Wicksell Lectures to suggest that between 1880 and 1913 dynamic gains, as well as allocational efficiency gains, resulted from trade throughout the tropics. McGreevey finds that trade was a dynamic factor in Colombian development after about 1890, and Lewis's students reach similar conclusions for other countries.[13] Most of the analyses mentioned so far are consistent with, and apparently drawn upon, the general descriptions just examined. In other words, almost everyone, leftists included, imagines that foreign demand for most LDC products boomed during the half-century before World War I and that external stimuli to economic development in the LDCs were potentially strong.

Given the consensus that world demand for most LDC products was

---

[11]Hla Myint, "The Gains from International Trade and the Backward Countries," in H. Myint, *Economic Theory and the Underdeveloped Countries* (New York: Oxford University Press, 1971). By "dynamic benefits" Myint and others mean not only specialization and division of labor but also such things as transfer of technology and entrepreneurship, capital inflows, and economies of scale that may be obtained by backward societies as they enter international commerce and that may lead to self-sustaining growth or enhance the prospects for such growth.

[12]N. Leff, "Tropical Trade and Development in the Nineteenth Century: The Brazilian Experience," *Journal of Political Economy* 81 (May/June 1973): 678–696; J. Levin, *The Export Economies* (Cambridge, Mass.: Harvard University Press, 1960); J. R. Mandle, *The Plantation Economy* (Philadelphia: Temple University Press, 1974).

[13]W. P. McGreevey, *An Economic History of Colombia, 1845–1930* (London: Cambridge University Press, 1971); Lewis, ed., *Tropical Development*.

expansive, differences in interpretation usually reflect different perceptions of the internal linkages between external stimuli and domestic economic performance. Perhaps the leading theoretical contribution is Baldwin's export technology hypothesis, the inspiration for several case studies.[14] Baldwin maintains that under certain conditions the production function of the commodity or commodities a region first exports sets the pattern for the region's future development. In general, labor-intensive plantation crops, such as cane sugar, are growth-retarding, whereas nonplantation crops, such as wheat, are growth-promoting. Other problems that may exist regardless of whether a particular economy is organized around plantations are a parasitical class of luxury importers, bad colonial government, the tendency of foreign entrepreneurs to repatriate profits earned from exports, and economic and social traditionalism on the part of the indigenous population.

Nevertheless, evidence of rational economic behavior and flexible response to opportunity in many parts of the Third World is abundant. Hill's work on the migrant cocoa farmers of Ghana and Morris's work on the recruitment of an industrial labor force in nineteenth-century India are particularly commendable.[15] Modern investigations of peasant agriculture also indicate that the farmer in the Third World is a prime example of economic man.[16] Lewis, for one, weights this evidence more heavily than evidence of economic rigidities in assessing the historical situation faced by impoverished nations.

Leff makes an analysis that is different from most of those mentioned so far.[17] He argues that Brazil reaped few dynamic gains from trade during the nineteenth century despite the presence of favorable internal conditions. In his view, it was the small export sector and slow export growth, especially in per capita terms, that constrained the naturally dynamic response of the Brazilian economy. The attention given to feeble external stimuli instead of indigenous obstacles to resource reallocation is refreshing, but whether the conclusions can be applied to the entire less developed world is problematical, as Leff admits.

---

[14]R. Baldwin, "Patterns of Development in Newly Settled Regions," *Manchester School of Economic and Social Studies* 24 (May 1956): 161–179. See also G. L. Beckford, *Persistent Poverty* (London: Oxford University Press, 1972).

[15]P. Hill, *The Migrant Cocoa-Farmers of Southern Ghana: A Study in Rural Capitalism* (Cambridge: Cambridge University Press, 1963); M. D. Morris, *The Emergence of an Industrial Labor Force in India: A Study of the Bombay Cotton Mills, 1854–1947* (Berkeley: University of California Press, 1965).

[16]See T. W. Schultz, *Transforming Traditional Agriculture* (New Haven: Yale University Press, 1964).

[17]Leff, "Tropical Trade: Brazilian Experience."

Though brief, this review of the analytical literature raises a host of empirical questions. How large were exports in relation to national product in the LDCs? How rapid was per capita export growth? What proportion of aggregate LDC exports was represented by commodities with growth-retarding production functions? How many LDCs specialized in such commodities? Did these goods occupy a larger or smaller position in the trade of the nations that produced them as the nineteenth century elapsed? This book answers some, though not all, of these questions, thus making possible further refinement of existing theories about the historical relationship between foreign trade and economic development in the Third World.

It is appropriate to anticipate a few of the major conclusions. On the descriptive level, it is found that the modern network of world trade had been largely formed by 1860, that the rate of expansion of the aggregate volume of LDC exports was lower between 1860 and 1900 than during the previous several decades, that changes in the commodity composition of LDC exports were less profound after 1850 than is usually thought, and that there was a marked shift away from the United Kingdom and toward continental Europe and North America as the main outlets for LDC products as the nineteenth century progressed. For reasons given later in this book, it is very likely that for many LDCs the expansion of trade was not rapid enough to change economic conditions significantly, which helps explain why the diversification of exports was not more extensive. Furthermore, export sectors in the LDCs often were small, especially in midcentury, which contributed to the same general results. These findings complement and enhance other explanations of why the Victorian expansion of trade did relatively little to advance the prospects of most of Asia, Africa, and Latin America for rapid and continuing economic development.

Sources and Methods

Since the developing nations of the nineteenth century wanted to improve trading relations with other nations, including the "backward" ones, it was natural for them to inquire into the economic behavior of their potential trading partners. One outstanding collection of data is the *Statistical Abstract of Foreign Countries,* which was published in 1909 by the United States Department of Commerce and Labor and which contains import and export time series of varying lengths for some 60 countries. Many of the series are long, and the data are meticulously presented. The *Abstract* also depicts the composition of each country's exports by trading partners and commodities for later years. This source should not be confused with the

Statistical Abstract of Foreign Countries published annually by the Board of Trade of Great Britain. The latter publication provides some useful information on the LDCs but gives more attention to now-developed countries.

Another American source is the *Commercial Relations of the United States with Foreign Countries,* published from 1856 to 1912 by various departments and agencies of the federal government. After 1880, *Commercial Relations* became an annual survey of world trade. It included a description of the trade of every country for which relevant information could be obtained, relying primarily on consular reports that frequently estimated the level and composition of the foreign trade of countries not compiling official returns or having unreliable returns.

The remaining sources published in the United States are conveniently described as "Special Reports." From time to time, government agencies published studies of the trade of particular countries or of commodities entering international commerce. These are often associated with official trade returns but sometimes are separate and distinct.

American sources contain excellent data for the last quarter of the nineteenth century but are less informative about previous years. The colonial reports of other powers provide useful information on earlier trade, however. The English *Statistical Tables Relating to the Colonial and Other Possessions of the United Kingdom* is a prime example of such a report. The *Tables* were published annually by the Board of Trade and grew more comprehensive as the British Empire expanded. One useful feature of the *Tables* is that colonial exports were often classified by destination in both quantity and value terms. The *Tables* are summarized in the *Statistical Abstract of Colonies,* an annual publication throughout much of the century.

Two other remarkable English compendia are the *Tables Relating to Foreign Countries,* a compilation of comprehensive trade data for many countries and their colonies published at irregular intervals between 1830 and 1870 as a supplement to the main annual statistical summaries for the United Kingdom, and Macgregor's five-volume work *Commercial Statistics,* published in 1847. The Macgregor volumes summarize the trade history of every country in the world from about 1800 and especially from about 1830. Hundreds of tables from the official and unofficial records of various countries were reproduced in English.

The sources just described are nearly sufficient for the purposes of this research. Occasionally, reference is made to country and commodity studies or to such standard reference works as *The Statesman's Yearbook* and Mulhall's *Dictionary of Statistics.*

Most of the principal sources represent translations of records from various non-English-language countries. Conceivably, the data could have been reconstructed directly from the primary sources of each country, but this approach would have entailed a heartbreaking amount of work and might not have yielded more useful results than the translated compilations. The coverage here is, after all, quite comprehensive, ranging from 40 countries in 1840 to 91 countries in 1900. In any case, while researchers developing time series for individual countries from national data of the period or subsequently revised statistical series might obtain results different from those presented here, the sources that were relied on in this study have been neglected and, as will be shown, are extremely useful in working up a persuasive new view of the nineteenth-century network of world trade.

The argument might be made that because the data presumably contain large errors of measurement, they should be disregarded. The question, however, is not primarily whether the data are good, in terms of absolutes, but whether they compare well with the best alternative, the impressions of today's experts. Given the fact that presumably intelligent contemporaries did their best to measure economic flows during the nineteenth century, the burden of proof is on sceptics to justify dismissing this information. Furthermore, a good deal of expert opinion is based on these data, regardless of whether the debt is made explicit. It seems better to treat the evidence systematically than to rely on selective observations. Finally, given the political and economic objectives of today's LDCs, there is room for willful misinterpretation of the past for the sake of state or ideology. Chicanery is riskier when the actual historical data are conveniently available.

Having said this, it should be added that these data are unlikely to be seriously misleading. There are several reasons why:

1. Governments often had a vested interest in accurate data for tax reasons.
2. The numbers usually do not contradict well-founded impressions based on independent evidence.
3. Regular patterns often appear that are not plausibly attributed to chance or to systematic biases, especially since the data were collected and processed by many hands around the world.
4. Such idiosyncrasies as exist in the data are often obvious, and allowances can be made for them.
5. Excellent statistical work was done for the British colonies as far back as the 1830s.
6. Data collection was also in Western hands for several other countries, including China. For these particular components of LDC trade, measurement error is almost certainly small.

For statistical purposes, the world is divided into 10 regions:

1. United Kingdom
2. Other Western Europe
   Austria–Hungary
   Belgium
   Denmark
   France
   Germany
   Holland
   Italy
   Norway
   Sweden
   Switzerland
3. North America
   Canada
   United States
4. Oceania
5. Other Europe
   Bulgaria
   Finland
   Greece
   Portugal
   Roumania
   Russia
   Servia
   Spain
   Turkey
6. South America
7. Central America
   Central American Republics
   West Indies
   Mexico
8. Asia
9. Northern Africa
   Algeria
   Barbary States
   Egypt
10. Southern (or sub-Saharan) Africa

This system of classification is based on the accepted chronology of the onset and international diffusion of modern economic growth. One of its advantages is that it permits a test of the hypothesis that the effects on LDC trade of economic development in Great Britain and the later-arriving regions to growth were different. It is well known that Argentina, Cape of Good Hope, and Japan began to experience modern economic growth before 1900; they are therefore separated from neighboring countries when it is feasible and desirable to do so. Uruguay, a borderline case, is treated as an LDC. Africa is divided into two regions, in part because aggregating the sparse data available for this continent might lead to misleading conclusions. There also appear to have been differences in the timing of the entrance of the two regions of Africa into the international economy. Perhaps the same could be said of South America or Asia, but the contrasts in these regions seem to be less marked than in Africa. The region Other Europe might have been treated as a less developed area, but it was not feasible to study the exports of this region as thoroughly as those of other regions. Other Europe will therefore be noticed fleetingly.

For the purposes of this study, post-1840 developments in world and LDC trade are of particular interest, although data that were uncovered for the pre-1840 period are presented when necessary. The terminal date is 1900, although some later twentieth-century data are used for comparative purposes. One reason for stopping at 1900 was to avoid pointless overlapping with existing studies, especially *Forty Years of Foreign Trade*. A second reason is that the turn of the century came soon after the so-called Second Industrial Revolution. New influences on world trade accompanied the Second Industrial Revolution, so 1900 or thereabouts could easily have been an economic turning point. Furthermore, Leff's trend equations for Brazilian trade reveal three distinct periods before World War I, one of which is 1850–1896.

The exchange rates used to convert foreign currencies into dollars are listed in Appendix A. Often the conversions had been done in the source materials, although the rates of exchange employed were not usually specified. It was easy to determine, however, what the standard rates of exchange were at different times. A list of abbreviations of the titles of sources is also given in Appendix A. The export data are f.o.b. and usually refer to domestic merchandise. In a few cases the data refer to total exports and/or include exports of gold and silver.

Pre-1913 boundaries apply in all cases. It was not possible to adjust the data for changes in boundaries during the nineteenth century, but there is no reason to believe that there would be any appreciable effect on the results obtained, especially those at a high level of aggregation. For stylistic purposes, the terms Great Britain and British will usually be taken to mean the United Kingdom as a whole, that is, England, Wales, Scotland, and Ireland.

Finally, a word of warning. Anyone who works with LDC trade data for the nineteenth century must often grope in the dark, and it is easy to commit the fallacy of misplaced precision. In general, the inferences drawn here can be defended even if the data contain a wide margin of error. Moreover, information supplied by other writers can be used to complete and embellish the picture. But no attempt is made to force the data into falsely consistent patterns or to explain differences with other writers, of which there happily are only a few. At this preliminary level of analysis, we must be satisfied with general patterns and accept that some nuances will escape detection and minor inconsistencies occasionally crop up.

2
Trends in Nineteenth-Century Trade

Growth Rates

Although the nineteenth century witnessed a remarkable expansion in world trade, the rate of growth was lower then than it has been since World War II. Rates of growth in international trade are harder to measure the farther back one goes in time, but independent estimates made by scholars using different methods always lead to this conclusion. Table 2.1, for example, presents two sets of estimates of the growth rate of world trade during several time spans between 1800 and the recent past. The first set of estimates was prepared especially for this book using a new procedure described in the note to Table 2.1; the second is more traditional. It is based on familiar data recently reinterpreted by W. W. Rostow. Although the discrepancies between the two series are indicative of the difficulties involved in describing historical trends in international trade, the patterns in each series are similar. After the Napoleonic Wars the rate of growth increased markedly. Peaking in midcentury, the rate subsequently fell but remained at a historically high level until rising again in the first decade of the twentieth century. After the catastrophic dislocations brought on by two global wars and a worldwide depression, it hit still another new high in the postwar period.

Exports from the LDCs grew at roughly the same rate as world exports during most of the nineteenth century, and the growth rates of both declined sharply from midcentury levels toward the end of the century. Actually, the data in Appendix A, when deflated by Imlah's index of British import prices, suggest that the rate of growth of LDC exports was about 3.9% per year during the peak period 1840–1860, as compared with the rate of

TABLE 2.1

Estimated Annual Average Compound Rates of Growth in Volume of World Trade, 1800–1970 (percent per year)

Period	Hanson	Rostow	
1800–1820	1.8	1.5	
1820–1840	4.0	2.8	
1840–1860	5.6	4.8	
1860–1880	4.3	3.9	
1876/1880–1896/1900	3.0	3.3	
1896/1900–1911/1913	4.2	4.4	
1911/1913–1926/1929	1.1	.7	(1913–1929)
1926/1929–1936/1938	−.3	−1.2	(1929–1938)
1936/1938–1953/1958	3.0	3.0	
1953–1966	7.0	7.3	(1953–1967)
1960–1970	9.0	8.2	(1958–1971)

Source: Calculations described in note to this table and W. W. Rostow (1978, pp. 67, 669).

Note: The estimates for the value of world trade in current prices, from which the volume indices were constructed, are taken from several sources. For the years 1800 through 1840, the source was Day (1922), adjusted slightly according to procedures suggested by Imlah (1958). For the year 1840, Day's estimate is in close agreement with my independent one. The estimates for 1860 and 1880 are my own, but they are close to those supplied by Kuznets and Yates. From 1880 to 1953/1955 I have used the sophisticated estimates of world trade in constant dollars given by Yates to estimate the annual growth rates in trade volumes, although my data give similar results for overlapping periods. The final estimates are taken from the General Agreement on Tariffs and Trade.

There are several procedures that can be used to adjust the value data for price level changes. Kuznets uses the Rousseaux index to deflate his long-term series of world trade values. The Rousseaux index is mainly an index of wholesale food and raw material prices in the United Kingdom during the century, and its main virtue is that it covers a long period of time. Another procedure, which I favor, is to subtract British exports from estimated world exports and to deflate the former with an index of British export prices and the remainder with an index of British import prices. Imlah has provided us with these indices for all of the nineteenth century. This method, although not ideal, has both theoretical and practical advantages over Kuznets's method. It comes closer to deflating each component of world trade by an index appropriate to that component and, because Great Britain's trade relations were so extensive, British imports are as unbiased a sample of non-British exports as one is likely to find. I also tried to break world trade at various sample dates into even finer components, by either countries or goods, when I found relevant price indexes for these components, but the results were not significantly different from the method just described. The basic contrast, then, is between the Rousseaux method and the British export–import price method.

Applying the two methods to the same data for sample dates 20 years apart yielded different results for the periods 1820–1840 and 1880–1900. The Rousseaux method gave lower estimates of the rate of growth of world trade during those intervals. Because of the theoretical advantages of the other method, the higher estimates were chosen. Nonetheless, both methods lead to essentially the same inferences about long-term trends.

roughly 5% for the world as a whole. But this contrast is misleading, because the 1840 data do not cover several large European countries, listed later in this chapter, for which the appropriate data are available in 1860. Thus, the growth rates of non-LDC exports and world trade computed from these data are too high. Similarly, several LDCs that are represented in the 1840 data (e.g., Cuba) are omitted in the 1860 data, with the result that the growth rate estimated for LDC exports in midcentury is too low. But none of this changes the conclusion that the last part of the nineteenth century witnessed a significant decline in the growth rates of world and LDC trade as compared with earlier decades.

Although the availability of data and the other purposes of this study governed the selection of benchmark dates, the conclusions reached by scholars taking other approaches are consistent with the portrayal given so far. Bairoch's exhaustive analysis of trends in the value and volume of European exports, which amounted to more than 60% of world exports during the nineteenth century, reveals three phases of growth before 1900.[1] During the first, 1815/1820–1845/1847, the volume of European exports grew at rates of 3–4% per year; during the second phase, 1845/1847–1873/1875, the annual rate of growth was between 4.5 and 5% per year; during the last phase, 1873/1875–1900, the rate was only 2.5% per year.

Kuznets puts the rate of growth of world trade at about 60% per decade (5% per year) between 1840 and 1860 and at a little better than 30% per decade (3% per year) between 1880 and 1900. The estimates in Yates's *Forty Years of Foreign Trade* suggest that the growth rate of aggregate LDC exports in the final quarter of the nineteenth century was also on the order of 3% per year, and Crafts has argued that the period 1880–1913 should be split into two periods for both world and LDC trade so that the depressed conditions in the world economy lasting until the mid-1890s and the buoyant conditions between then and World War I can be more easily distinguished.[2]

In a different context, Nugent provides a list of growth rates in the value of exports between the mid-1870s and mid-1890s for 56 LDCs.[3] The unweighted mean of these rates is 2.2% per year. World prices, however, were

[1]P. Bairoch, "European Foreign Trade in the XIX Century: The Development of the Value and Volume of Exports," *Journal of European Economic History* 2 (Spring 1973): 5–36; P. Bairoch, "Geographical Structure and Trade Balance of European Foreign Trade from 1800 to 1970," *Journal of European Economic History* 3 (Winter 1974): 557–608.

[2]S. Kuznets, "Level and Structure of Foreign Trade: Long-Term Trends," *Economic Development and Cultural Change* 15 (Jan. 1967): 1–140; N. F. R. Crafts, "Trade as a Handmaiden of Growth: An Alternative View," *Economic Journal* 83 (Sept. 1973): 875–884.

[3]J. B. Nugent, "Exchange-Rate Movements and Economic Development in the Late Nineteenth Century," *Journal of Political Economy* 81 (Sept./Oct. 1973): 1110–1135.

declining 2% per year, which means that the volume of exports for the average LDC grew faster than 2% per year. Perhaps the true rate was greater than 4% per year. Although this adjustment would not imply the occurrence of a late-century retardation in the growth rate of LDC exports, neither would it suggest buoyancy in comparison with preceding decades.

Furthermore, even though a weighted average of export growth rates in the LDCs during the period covered by Nugent would be hard to construct, a weighted average surely would tell another story. The unweighted average is unduly influenced by the data pertaining to smaller exporters and countries in their period of opening to international trade, such as French Guinea (18.8% per annum), New Caledonia (6.9%), Korea (16.9%), Nicaragua (5.8%), and Costa Rica (7.4%). In fact, 19 countries saw the value of exports decline, and such well-established members of the network of trade as Ceylon (1%), China (.5%), British India (1.7%), Mauritius (.3%), and Venezuela (1.2%) experienced low rates of growth. The median rate of growth for the 56 countries was 1.1% per year. Were it possible to measure accurately rates of export growth in real terms for these countries late-century sluggishness would still be indicated.

Most countries evidently did not experience an export boom during the late nineteenth century, and retardation seems to have been the normal condition. Additional evidence to the same effect will be introduced later. Perhaps some nations managed to buck the trend, but at a minimum the conventional assertion that world and LDC exports flourished near the end of the nineteenth century requires a great deal of qualification.

Network of World Trade

Existing accounts of how the network of trade evolved implicitly refer to a list of the countries that belonged to the network of world trade at various points in time during the nineteenth century, but no such list is available. Table 2.2 is a rudimentary but nonetheless enlightening attempt to fill this gap. Members of the trading community in the years 1820, 1840, 1860, 1880, and 1900 are listed in this table. As a general rule, no country was included unless it had exports of at least $2 million. One reason for selecting this criterion was that data on exports actually produced within a country (special exports) could not always be obtained. Moreover, it was not always obvious whether a given piece of data referred to special exports or included re-exports (special exports + re-exports = general exports). Some criterion had to be used to distinguish entrepôts, such as Hong Kong, from other participants in the network of world trade. A second reason was that it seemed reasonable to require that the exports of a given country be a non-negligible fraction of world trade in one or more items of merchandise. When no data on the value of a country's exports were available, other evidence, which had to be subjectively interpreted, was relied on.

Table 2.2 refers to the latest date by which a country or region had entered the network of trade. It could be argued that some countries, such as Mexico, were part of the network of trade before 1820; not coincidentally, the modern trend in historical studies of specific economies is to begin before 1850. Nevertheless, we do not need to delve into the fine points of dating for particular countries in order to make useful statements about the entire world economy.

Table 2.2 indicates that since the now-developed nations were completing the process of entry into the network of trade by 1820, the nucleus of the modern network of world trade had been formed by that time. By contrast, countries in Asia, Africa, South America, Central America, and Other Europe, the laggards with respect to modern economic growth, continued to join throughout the century. Moreover, some LDCs, such as Egypt, that belonged to the trading community in 1820 subsequently underwent such marked changes that they could be described as reentering the network of trade. But, these considerations notwithstanding, Table 2.2 indicates that entry into the modern network of world trade had nearly been completed by 1860. Tropical Africa was the main probable addition after that.

Shares in World Trade

Another way of appraising the position of the LDCs in world trade is to examine the shares of major regions in world exports. This information is displayed for four benchmark dates between 1840 and 1900 in Table 2.3. Before examining the table it should be mentioned that 1840 trade values were missing for Denmark, Italy, Norway, and Switzerland from Other Western Europe, and for Turkey from Other Europe. Consequently, the shares of these two regions are underestimated in the first column of the table and the shares of the other regions, overestimated. Bearing this in mind, it is probably correct to say that, appearances notwithstanding, the shares of Great Britain and North America in trade were stable or growing in the middle decades of the century and that the share of Other Western Europe was stable or falling. But after about 1860, Other Western Europe's share rose and Britain's share fell, while North America's share continued to rise.

The shares of Other Europe and possibly Central America fell after 1840, but the shares of other underdeveloped regions either rose or remained about the same. The decline in Asia's share is more apparent than real,

TABLE 2.2
Principal Nations Participating in World Trade in 1820 and Later Additions through 1900

1820	1840	1860	1880	1900
Europe				
Austria–Hungary	Roumania	Bulgaria		
Belgium		Finland		
Denmark		Greece		
France		Servia		
Germany				
Italy				
Netherlands				
Norway				
Portugal				
Russia				
Spain				
Sweden				
Switzerland				
Turkey				
United Kingdom				
North America				
Canada				
United States				
Central America				
Cuba		British Honduras		
Puerto Rico		Costa Rica		

Haiti		Guatemala	Paraguay
Santo Domingo		Honduras	
British West Indies		Nicaragua	
French West Indies		San Salvador	
Mexico		Dutch West Indies	

South America

Argentina	Dutch Guiana	Bolivia	
Brazil	Peru	Colombia	
British Guiana	Uruguay	Ecuador	
Chile	Venezuela		

Asia

British India	Ceylon	Indochina	Korea
China	Straits Settlements	Japan	
Dutch East Indies	Turkey in Asia	Persia	
Philippines		Siam	

Africa

Egypt	Cape of Good Hope	Algeria	Canary Islands
Mauritius		Barbary States	Tropical Africa
		Senegal	
		Zanzibar	

Oceania

	Australia	New Zealand	Fiji

Miscellaneous

		Hawaii	

TABLE 2.3
Shares in World Exports by Region, 1840–1900 (percentage)

Region	1840	1860	1880	1900
United Kingdom	22	21	17	14
Other Western Europe	33	39	40	41
Other Europe	9	9	8	7
North America	12	11	14	16
Central America	5	2	2	2
South America	5	5	5	5
Northern Africa	<1	<1	1	1
Southern Africa	<1	1	1	1
Asia	12	10	10	9
Oceania	<1	3	2	2

Source: Computed from tables in Appendix A.
Note: Columns may not total 100 because of rounding. Figures for 1860 and 1880 for Central America are estimates.

because of the problems with the data pertaining to 1840. The combined shares of Africa, Asia, and South America amounted to 18% in 1840 and 16% in 1900, according to Table 2.3, which implies that the rate of growth of exports from these areas largely conformed to the rate of growth of world trade as a whole. In other words, these regions began their trade expansion early, but the rate of growth of their exports, like the rate of growth of world trade as a whole, was neither constant nor as high as in the postwar period.

Economic Interdependence

It is important to know how the degree of interdependence among the various parts of the world changed as the international economy expanded. One indicator of economic interdependence is trade per capita in the world as a whole and in separate regions. A better measure of interdependence with respect to income, but not price, changes is the share of trade in total output.[4] Because the few existing estimates of nineteenth-century national product refer mainly to advanced countries, computation of the ratio of trade or exports to national product for specific LDCs is usually impossible. Zimmerman, however, provides historical estimates of total and per capita income in constant prices for several large regions.[5] The geographic cover-

[4]See R. D. Tollison and T. D. Willett, "International Integration and the Interdependence of Economic Variables," *International Organization* 27 (Spring 1974): 255–272.
[5]L. J. Zimmerman, "The Distribution of World Income, 1860–1900," in *Essays on Unbalanced Growth*, ed. E. DeVries (The Hague: Mouton & Co., 1962), pp. 52–53.

age of his data is incomplete, and his estimates begin only in 1860, but they are still helpful in estimating the share of exports in national product in Asia, South America, and Other Europe at several dates within the Victorian period.

Estimates of trade per capita in constant dollars for several regions at several benchmark dates are displayed in Table 2.4. They include, of course, intraregional trade as well as interregional trade. Except for the entry in the first cell, the 1820 column was derived inferentially by a procedure described in the note to Table 2.4. Also described there are the method of eliminating the influence of changes in the general price level and the population figures used. The 1820 numbers are conjectural, but the others are based on actual trade data and indicate the degree of commitment of the various regions to trade at points in time and changes over time. These

TABLE 2.4
Per Capita Exports from Selected Regions, 1820–1900
(in constant dollars; 1880 = 100) [a]

Region	1820	1840	1860	1880	1900
World	$ .45	$ .80	$ 2.10	$ 4.40	$ 7.55
United Kingdom	3.65	7.25	20.70	31.00	36.25
Other Western Europe	1.70	2.90	7.30	14.80	25.90
Other Europe	.85	1.25	2.80	4.30	5.95
North America	3.00	5.15	8.85	18.95	26.80
Central America [b]	n.a.	5.55	n.a.	n.a.	8.85
South America	1.05	2.00	5.60	9.10	15.05
Asia	.05	.15	.35	.80	1.30
Africa	.05	.10	.45	1.55	2.40
Oceania	n.a.	2.50	n.a.	n.a.	46.35

Source: Calculations described in note to this table and Appendix A.

[a] Numbers rounded to nearest nickel.

[b] Figures for Central America indicate current values.

Note: The population estimates used in constructing this table came from several sources. The figures for the European countries for each date came from Sundbärg (1908). For the rest of the world (except Africa) the figures came from Zimmerman after 1860. The pre-1860 figures for the non-European world came from Durand (1966), whose estimates were interpolated by assuming an even rate of growth between his benchmark years. Since Durand combines Central and South America, two-thirds of his figures were allocated to South America and one-third to Central America before 1860. It should be noted that the totals of Zimmerman's estimates for the LDCs, which pertain to Latin America and Asia only, are within the margins of error of Durand's estimates for these regions. Durand's figures were used for Africa at all dates.

In deflating the value totals for each region, Imlah's index of United Kingdom import prices was used for every region but that nation and Central America. United Kingdom exports were deflated by Imlah's index of British export prices.

For the year 1820 it was assumed that each region had the same share in world exports that it had in 1840. This is a questionable assumption, but it probably leads to an overestimate of the 1820 shares of the LDCs. Thus, it makes the comparisons with later years less dramatic than they would be if lower figures were used and has the effect of strengthening the conclusions reached in the text.

estimates, incidentally, are consistent with Bairoch's estimates for Europe.[6]
The salient points of Table 2.4 are:

1. The large expansion in per capita trade for the world as a whole—almost 17-fold between 1820 and 1900. The base is low, however.
2. The high level of per capita exports in Great Britain, Other Western Europe, and North America at each date compared with Other Europe, South America, Asia, and Africa. Of the latter group, South America is especially high and Asia and Africa especially low.
3. The relative stagnation of Central America's per capita exports. That these are in current values probably is not misleading, since an index of the prices of Jamaican exports during the second half of the nineteenth century (see p. 58), which were comparatively diverse and probably are representative of Central American exports in general, fluctuated within a narrow range.
4. The rapid growth after 1860 of African exports per capita relative to Asian exports per capita.
5. In 1900 per capita exports in Asia and Africa were about the same as those in Other Western Europe in 1820. If the LDCs had reached the level of economic development that Other Western Europe had reached by 1820, the implication is that they were at least as dependent on trade as this now-developed region was earlier. If per capita incomes were lower in the LDCs in 1900 than in Other Western Europe in 1820, the LDC export–national-product ratio in 1900 would have been greater than the earlier one for Other Western Europe.

This line of inquiry can be extended using Zimmerman's estimates of per capita income in several regions in conjunction with the estimates of per capita exports in Table 2.4 to derive estimates of the share of exports in regional product. The results of dividing exports by income are given in Table 2.5, which also presents Kuznets's estimates of export proportions for several advanced countries at comparable dates. Before examining this table, it must be cautioned that this exercise yields only suggestive results. Several statistical problems in reconciling the export and income estimates are described in the note to Table 2.5. Furthermore, estimates of national income in the underdeveloped world during the nineteenth century presumably are subject to significant error. Nevertheless, Zimmerman's estimates are based on intensive and comprehensive research that makes use of some of the best independent empirical work. In a few cases Zimmerman's estimates are based on direct communication with foreign governments. Its

[6]Bairoch, "European Foreign Trade."

TABLE 2.5

Share of Exports in National Product for Selected Countries and Regions, 1820–1900 (percentage)

Region	1820	1840	1860	1880	1900
United Kingdom	10.0	9.0	16.0	16.0	13.0
France	7.0	7.0	16.0	24.0	24.0
Germany	n.a.	7.0	n.a.	16.0	13.0
United States	6.6	6.2	6.2	6.8	6.7
Other Europe	n.a.	n.a.	4.9	5.3	6.0
South America	n.a.	n.a.	10.0	14.0	18.0
Asia	n.a.	n.a.	1.0	2.1	4.6
Jamaica[a]	43.5	24.3	20.2	19.1	22.6

Source: Developed countries, Kuznets (1967); LDCs, see p. 22; Jamaica, Eisner (1961, p. 237).

[a] The figures for Jamaica are for a decade later than indicated by column heading.

Note: The main problem in compiling this table is that Zimmerman says little about his method of adjusting for secular changes in price levels other than that his per capita income estimates are expressed in dollars of 1953. The estimates of exports per capita in Table 2.4 are in dollars of 1880; they are therefore not directly comparable with Zimmerman's income estimates.

It was possible, however, to make these export estimates compatible with Zimmerman's income estimates by the following procedure. Zimmerman's estimates of British per capita income in 1860, 1880, and 1900 were multiplied by accepted estimates of the share of exports in Great Britain's national product for those dates prepared by Kuznets, thereby obtaining estimates of British per capita exports in dollars of 1953. Then, after taking the ratios at each date of the per capita exports of Asia, South America, and Other Europe in dollars of 1880 to Great Britain's per capita exports in dollars of 1880, estimated British per capita exports in dollars of 1953 were multiplied by these ratios to get estimates of the per capita exports of Asia, South America, and Other Europe in dollars of 1953. The ratios of these estimates and Zimmerman's per capita income estimates were then taken to get the estimated shares of exports in the total products of Asia, South America, and Other Europe. Because Zimmerman's data are highly aggregated, it was impossible to disaggregate the geographic classifications any further.

weaknesses notwithstanding, the Zimmerman survey is an immensely valuable summary of information on national incomes in the Third World during the nineteenth century.

If we start with the middle of Table 2.5, the post-1860 upsurge in the export–national-product ratio for Asia and South America stands out. The increases are substantial, and although Africa is missing from the table, the increase for that region must have been substantial also. As noted in Table 2.4, Africa forged past Asia in per capita exports during this period, and per capita income in Africa probably was no higher than in Asia. It could have been lower. The export proportion for Other Europe shows a slow rise beginning in 1860.

There are other reasons why these estimates are plausible. Exports from the LDCs grew faster than 4% per year in real terms between 1840 and 1880 and at about 3% per year between 1880 and 1900. A failure of export proportions to rise would mean that real product in the LDCs was growing at least at the same rates as exports—rates that would be respectable even for the industrial countries. Although Zimmerman's estimates are only rough approximations, the growth rate of real product in the LDCs presumably was not this high during the nineteenth century. Hence, exports must have been an increasing share of total product in these regions.

Another striking feature of Table 2.5 is South America's comparatively high export proportion at each date. The estimate for this region in 1900 also is consistent with the earliest estimate for Brazil, given by Leff.[7] According to Leff's study, exports averaged 18% of Brazilian national product between 1920 and 1924, which is exactly the same as the estimate given in Table 2.5 for all of South America in 1900. Although Leff adds that the true figure for Brazil may have been as low as 10%, it seems fair to say that with the exception of a few so-called export economies (e.g., Jamaica) only South America among the underdeveloped regions had an export–national-product ratio that approached the ratios of the now-developed European countries as the twentieth century began.

The differences between South America and Asia in the share of output devoted to exports are surprisingly wide. The estimates for Asia seem low, but China, a huge country with little interest in trade, is included in the figures. For British India, the ratio of exports to national product hit its all-time high of only 11% in 1913, according to Maddison.[8] Although large differences exist within Asia, the generalization that Asia exported a smaller proportion of its total product than did other less developed regions remains true.

The likely direction of bias in the estimates should also be mentioned. Since the proportion of economic activity reflected in market transactions is much lower in the LDCs than in the now-developed countries and since this presumably was as true in the nineteenth century as it is today, Zimmerman's national income estimates are likely to be low. Indeed, given the importance of subsistence agriculture in these predominantly agricultural societies, the estimates could be very low. The trade figures in the numerator are unlikely to have any omissions of comparable magnitude; rather, they may be high because of the inclusion of re-exports in the basic figures for some countries. Thus, the low estimates given above may actually *overstate* the true ratios of exports to national product in the LDCs during the nineteenth century.

[7]N. Leff, "Tropical Trade and Development in the Nineteenth Century: The Brazilian Experience," *Journal of Political Economy* 81 (May/June 1973): 690.

[8]A. Maddison, *Class Structure and Economic Growth* (New York: W. W. Norton & Co., 1971), p. 59.

A Disaggregate View

Aggregate estimates, such as those presented in the previous section, conceal a great deal of detail. Ours, moreover, cannot be very exact even in their own terms. It is therefore useful to take a look at specific LDCs for which more reliable data exist, a procedure that permits a comparison of the micro and macro pictures. Doing this also makes possible a test of the general applicability of the Leff hypothesis. According to this hypothesis, the combination of slow growth in per capita exports and small export sectors explains the failure of Brazil and other LDCs to obtain sizable dynamic gains from trade during the nineteenth century.

Table 2.6 contains estimates of per capita exports in a large sample of LDCs for the years 1860, 1880, 1900, and 1913; Table 2.7 contains estimates of growth rates of per capita exports in these countries during two intervals of time, 1860–1900 and 1900–1913. These time periods do not correspond exactly to the 1850–1896 and 1897–1913 periods which Leff examines, in part because data going back to 1850 are insufficient for our purposes. Furthermore, Leff based his time periods on residuals from trend equations estimated for Brazil alone. It is enough for the estimates to span a long period of time, to be widely spaced chronologically, and to permit subdivision of the whole period into reasonably homogeneous segments. In keeping with the spirit of Leff's article, the period 1860–1900 is analyzed. The procedures used to prepare the estimates are described in the notes to Tables 2.6 and 2.7.

Brazil in International Perspective

On one reading, the evidence presented in Tables 2.6 and 2.7 fails to support Leff's conjecture. Taking the level of per capita exports as a proxy for the share of exports in national product (an unavoidable oversimplification), Brazil was merely an "average" LDC according to Table 2.6. Per capita exports in Brazil were at or above the median of the sample in 1860 and 1900 but were below the mean at each of those dates. According to Table 2.7, the Brazilian rate of per capita export growth was below the LDC average whether the mean or the median is taken as the standard of comparison.

An interpretation more favorable to Leff is possible if Table 2.6 is read in relation to Table 2.7. Only two countries with high per capita exports in 1860—Costa Rica and Uruguay—experienced a rate of per capita export growth higher than Brazil's. Jamaica, Puerto Rico, British Guiana, and Peru witnessed an actual decline in per capita exports. By contrast, several countries, such as Honduras and Nicaragua, experienced rapid export growth

TABLE 2.6

Per Capita Exports from Selected Countries, 1860–1913 (three-year average, in dollars)[a]

Country	1860	1880	1900	1913
Central America				
Costa Rica	(15.00)	(10.50)	28.41	(33.33)
Cuba	(18.00)	n.a.	33.21	(65.60)
Guatemala	(1.90)	n.a.	(4.69)	(7.78)
Honduras	(1.50)	n.a.	(11.80)	(8.34)
Jamaica	13.79	10.44	12.62	n.a.
Mexico	n.a.	3.00	5.42	n.a.
Nicaragua	(.75)	n.a.	5.60	(13.34)
Puerto Rico	(9.16)	n.a.	(7.33)	n.a.
South America				
Brazil	5.90	7.18	8.94	(12.37)
British Guiana	47.41	52.70	33.78	n.a.
Chile	13.62	22.44	20.96	(41.43)
Colombia	3.60	8.40	4.10	(5.68)
Ecuador	(3.00)	(4.63)	(8.56)	(16.00)
Peru	(9.96)	(7.14)	5.66	(9.77)

(continued)

Source: Calculations described in note to this table; see also Hanson (1976).

[a] Parentheses indicate estimate pertains to year at column head or nearby year. Figure for Cuba in Column 1 is based on 1842 data, and figure in Column 3 is 3-year average centered on 1901; for Colombia, annual averages, 1855–1859, 1875–1879, and 1895–1899, are taken from McGreevey (1971, p. 104); for Uruguay, Column 1 figure is 3-year average centered on 1864; for Venezuela, 3-year averages are centered on 1854, 1876, and 1894; for Ceylon, annual averages for decades 1860–1869, 1880–1889, 1900–1909, and 1910–1919 are taken from Lim (1968, p. 248); for China, first figure is 3-year average centered on 1865; for Dutch East Indies, 1860 export data come from Furnivall (1939, p. 170); and for Siam first figure is 3-year average centered on 1869, whereas 1913 export data come from Maddison (1971, p. 59). Other export data for 1913 are taken from Yates (1959, p. 239). The estimates in the table are refinements of ones presented in Hanson (1976) and where possible refer to special exports.

Note: Most of the export data are taken from the U.S. *Statistical Abstract of Foreign Countries*, whereas most of the population data are taken from Zimmerman's list. However, for China's population Durand's estimates were used. For British Guiana and Egypt, which are not listed by Zimmerman, the sources were Mandle (1974) and Issawi (1961). Because of the lack of reliable population data for most of Africa, only one country from this region, Egypt is included in Table 2.6. However, Durand gives aggregate population estimates for sub-Saharan Africa in the nineteenth century, and in order to obtain at least a rough impression of the degree of involvement of Tropical Africa in trade during this period, I have used his "medium" estimates in conjunction with the export data in Appendix A to calculate per capita exports for that region in 1860 and 1900. The results of these calculations are presented in Table 2.6 but are not included in subsequent statistical comparisons, although taken at face value they would strengthen the argument.

Whenever possible, 3-year averages of the export data centered on the benchmark years were used in computing the per capita figures. When a 1-year export figure was the only one available, the estimate using that figure is denoted in Table 2.6 by parentheses. I have not followed Leff in deflating the export data to

TABLE 2.6 (*continued*)

Country	1860	1880	1900	1913
Uruguay	17.80	27.61	35.89	(65.45)
Venezuela	3.33	7.10	8.77	(12.18)
Asia				
British India	.63	1.06	1.26	(2.73)
Ceylon	7.78	5.83	9.72	(18.95)
China	.18	.24	.29	n.a.
Dutch East Indies	1.77	2.47	2.53	(5.61)
Philippines	(2.00)	3.62	2.77	(5.74)
Siam	1.06	1.32	2.26	(5.18)
Africa				
Egypt	(3.49)	10.00	8.12	(13.08)
Tropical Africa	(.33)	n.a.	(1.00)	n.a.
Mean (excluding Tropical Africa)	8.27	10.32	11.42	19.03
Median (excluding Tropical Africa)	3.60	7.14	8.12	12.37

estimate long-term trends in the income terms of trade. Price indexes of imports are available for too few LCDs to make this procedure feasible, and it would be pointless to adjust the date for most or all of the countries surveyed by the Imlah index of British export prices, as Leff does for Brazil, since an across-the-board adjustment would not affect international comparisons. Also, presenting the data in unadjusted form gives the estimates greater flexibility for other scholarly purposes.

In this connection, it is worth pointing out that different observers can reach different conclusions about such apparently simple matters as total and per capita exports. An anonymous reviewer has supplied me with data for Mexico based on published Mexican sources, which I have compared with my data in the table at the end of this note. Both sets of estimates include exports of precious metals and are 1-year estimates only. The differences in the two sets of estimates are not trivial, but at least the estimates are close, and inferences drawn from either set would be similar.

	Total exports (millions of dollars)	Per capita exports (dollars)
1880		
Hanson	29.7	3.09
Reviewer	36.5	3.61
1900		
Hanson	74.6	5.49
Reviewer	78.4	5.76

TABLE 2.7
Compound Growth Rates of Per Capita Exports from Selected Countries,
1860–1900 and 1900–1913 (percent per year)

Country	1860–1900	1900–1913
Central America		
Costa Rica	1.6	2.2
Cuba	1.0	5.9
Guatemala	2.3	4.0
Honduras	5.3	−2.5
Jamaica	−.2	n.a.
Nicaragua	5.1	6.9
Puerto Rico	−.5	n.a.
South America		
Brazil	1.1	2.4
British Guiana	−.9	n.a.
Chile	1.1	5.4
Colombia	.3	2.1
Ecuador	2.6	4.9
Peru	−1.4	4.3
Uruguay	2.0	4.8
Venezuela	2.4	1.8
Asia		
British India	1.8	6.2
Ceylon	.6	6.9
China	1.2	n.a.
Dutch East Indies	.9	6.3
Philippines	.7	5.8
Siam	2.0	6.2
Africa		
Egypt	2.1	3.7
Mean	1.4	4.3
Median	1.2	4.9

Source: Table 2.6.

but began the period with low exports per capita. The same is probably true of many countries in Tropical Africa.[9] For the complete sample of LDCs (excluding Tropical Africa), the Spearman coefficient of rank correlation between the rate of per capita export growth during the 1860–1900 period and the level of per capita exports in 1860 is −.53, which is significant above the 5% confidence level.

[9]The sugar islands of Mauritius and Reunion probably are exceptions to this statement. These islands were similar to parts of the Caribbean and probably had high ratios of exports to national product and low rates of per capita export growth.

The point may be stated succinctly. An analysis of growth failure that is based on the combination of a low rate of per capita export growth and a small export sector is probably not applicable to most LDCs before 1900. It *is* likely, however, that most LDCs had at least one of these characteristics. Even this weaker statement is sufficient to establish the presumption that significant economic development would have been difficult for impoverished nations to achieve through expanding exports even if good domestic linkages between foreign trade and economic development had existed.

The Postbellum American South: Another Example

Recent work on economic retardation in the postbellum South lends further support to this conclusion. The similarities between the postbellum South and the LDCs are many and obvious. The southern standard of living was lower than that of the rest of the United States and of Western Europe, although it was not as low as that of the LDCs. The southern economy was primarily agricultural, it exported one product of consequence—cotton— and it was attuned to developments in foreign markets. An attenuated version of the plantation system still existed in parts of the South, and the region was experiencing cultural and political disorientation resulting from contact between the indigenous population and powerful outsiders, including the military governors and carpetbaggers. From the point of view of the industrializing world, the South was politically and economically disorganized; from the point of view of any particular LDC, the situation in the South differed little from its own.

Yet there were also several contrasts between the South and most LDCs. The South's plantation class had lost most of its political and economic power, and an aggressive merchant class was emerging. In the underdeveloped parts of the world where plantations were dominant, the system hung on tenaciously. Human capital in the South must have been superior to that in most less developed areas. (Human capital refers to not only education and training but also orientation toward and experience with a market economy.) The South resembled Brazil in the sense that better linkages between internal development and external trade stimuli existed there than in most lagging regions.

Wright's econometric analysis of economic retardation in the postbellum South is in the same spirit as Leff's analysis of economic retardation in late-nineteenth-century Brazil.[10] According to Wright, lagging world, and especially British, demand for cotton was the immediate reason for the slow

---

[10]G. Wright, "Cotton Competition and the Post-Bellum Recovery of the American South," *Journal of Economic History* 34 (Sept. 1974): 610–635.

recovery of southern incomes after the Civil War. Although this interpretation will be debated by students of American economic history for years to come, it is useful for our purposes because it throws the central question into sharp relief: Is it the quality of the internal linkages between development and trade that is at issue or is it the power of the external influence itself?

The attitude expressed in this book toward export-led economic development in most of Asia, Africa, and Latin America during the Victorian era is a modified version of Wright's toward the South: "The immediate impediment to [southern] recovery was lagging world cotton demand; deeper causes must be sought in the more traditional areas of southern institutions, investment patterns, and concentration on staple crops."[11]

Summary and Conclusions

The LDCs fully participated in the nineteenth-century expansion of world trade. Many LDCs entered the network of trade in the second quarter of the century, and the process of entry was nearly over by 1860. Only Tropical Africa among the major regions remained largely outside the community of trading nations by then. The LDCs more or less maintained their share of world trade as time went by, although the shares of most of the developing countries changed markedly. But for many LDCs the expansion of exports after 1860 was less impressive on a per capita basis than on a total basis.

As late as 1900 the LDCs still were less dependent on trade than today's developed countries. A so-called export economy like that of Jamaica exported only 20% of its national product, approximately the same percentage as France. Nevertheless, many LDCs exported increasing shares of their total product, whereas more advanced countries exported decreasing or stable shares. The decreasing self-sufficiency of the LDCs in the late nineteenth century also coincided with a decline in the rate of growth of world trade. But this is not really surprising or puzzling, since economic development in the less developed regions proceeded so slowly.

In general, these findings suggest that export growth in the late nineteenth century was less stimulative to economic development in the LDCs than many writers have supposed. Assuming, however, that the expansion of world and LDC trade was always rapid enough to propel growth under the right conditions, the trade "motor" still seems to have been small in relation to the task it was supposed to accomplish in the typical LDC—the economic advancement of the domestic subsistence sector. This is another instance of

[11]*Ibid.*, p. 610.

what McCloskey calls the "lemma of dispensability"—the idea that even large changes in a minor economic sector will have small consequences for national income. McCloskey's comment on the findings of the New Economic History in other contexts is also apt here: "It is no small matter to know that railways did not utterly dominate economic change in the nineteenth century; or that the tariff, however momentous its politics, was no magic key to economic change in German-speaking Europe."[12]

[12]D. McCloskey, "The Achievements of the Cliometric School," *ibid.*, 38 (Mar. 1978): 24–25.

3

Diversification and Concentration of Less Developed Countries' Exports

Introduction

A change in the commodity composition of a country's exports is often predicted to be one consequence of export-led economic development. According to the classical model, trade fosters internal specialization, division of labor, and other dynamic economic improvements, which in turn contribute to subsequent export diversification.[1] The Baldwin hypothesis, however, is focused on the technology used in the production of the commodity or commodities a region exports upon entering international trade. If the technology is not conducive to economic development, diversification of exports and other improvements would be slight, since structural change and resource reallocation would be impeded by technological and institutional conditions.[2]

Data on the commodity composition of exports and the degree of concentration of exports at different stages in a country's history are extremely useful to economists and historians. They are one indicator of the extent to which structural change occurred in the economy. In the now-developed countries and several currently developing countries, such as South Korea and Taiwan, economic development and changes in the composition of exports traditionally have been closely associated. It is possible, of course, that structural change will occur without being reflected in the commodity

[1]See W. A. Lewis, "The Export Stimulus," in *Tropical Development, 1880–1913,* ed. W. A. Lewis (Evanston, Ill.: Northwestern University Press, 1970); Douglass C. North, *The Economic Growth of the United States* (New York: W. W. Norton, 1966).

[2]See G. L. Beckford, *Persistent Poverty* (London: Oxford University Press, 1972); see also discussion of Baldwin in Chapter 1 of this volume.

composition of exports. Still, in the absence of other types of information, changes in the commodity composition and the degree of concentration of exports (or the lack thereof) offer clues to whether economic development is or was taking place.

Moreover, data on the commodity composition of exports and on the degree of concentration of exports in the LDCs during the nineteenth century can be combined with information about the production functions of various products to test the general and specific applicability of the Baldwin hypothesis. This hypothesis has proved useful in studies of several countries, but its general relevance remains open to question. It is by no means obvious that the common thread connecting most underdeveloped countries is the growth-inhibiting characteristics of their early exports. But only through careful examination of actual data can a scientific conclusion be reached.

Finally, data on the commodity composition of exports can help scholars to identify the markets that were most important to the LDCs during the nineteenth century and the main external forces that influenced LDC exports. Data on the commodity composition of exports also can be used to discover when and to what extent a particular country relied on especially unstable markets for foreign exchange earnings and whether ongoing export diversification contributed to a reduction in export instability. Although all of these issues cannot be adequately dealt with in a short book such as this, the data presented in this chapter at least enlarge the frame of reference within which these subjects may be discussed.

Diversification of Less Developed Countries' Exports

The approximate values in trade of the 22 largest exports by value from the LDCs in 1900, excluding precious metals, appear in Table 3.1. These values were calculated by summing the recorded value of exports of each good over the LDCs participating in each market. It is possible to trace the approximate values in trade for 14 of the top 22 goods back to 1840 and the values of the remaining 8 back to 1860.[3] Using the work of Stover, it also is possible to carry the table forward to 1913.[4] Approximate values of total LDC trade at each date are shown near the bottom of Table 3.1.[5]

[3] It might be argued that 3- or 5-year averages of the data rather than point estimates based on single years should be used. Unfortunately, the use of annual averages, though a nice refinement, is impractical given the sporadic nature of the data. Also, the wide spacing between benchmark dates reduces the possibility of errors arising from using data for single years only.

[4] C. Stover, "Tropical Exports," in *Tropical Development*, ed. Lewis, pp. 46–63.

[5] It should be noted that the estimated share in total LDC trade at each date of the goods listed in Table 3.1 is biased downward. First, many of the values of total exports of individual

Two common assertions about export diversification in the LDCs may be evaluated using Table 3.1. One is that export diversification (i.e., a growing list of exported products) was marked during the half-century or so before

---

countries include re-exports, which means that re-exports, including goods shipped from the now-developed countries, are incorporated into the combined totals of all LDC exports. There is, unfortunately, no way of knowing how much of the data is affected in this way, but it must be assumed that a significant bias is introduced. Second, flows of precious metals for balance of payments or other reasons were included in the official values of merchandise trade for several countries. If these could be removed from the total of LDC trade, the share of the goods listed in the table would rise. Third, the sporadic nature of the data for some countries made it necessary to exclude all or part of their exports from the table. The main omission is Cuba, a leading producer of sugar and tobacco. (But see just below.) In 1900 these goods accounted for most of Cuba's foreign exchange earnings, so that adding Cuba presumably would raise the share of the listed goods in LDC exports at each of the other dates. Also, the aggregate trade values for the whole Third World include other countries for which product-by-product breakdowns of exports were missing or incomplete. Thus, the values for trade in specific products given in the table typically underestimate the actual values, whereas the grand totals are closer to the mark.

It should also be noted that several categories in the table are general because the primary data often are not disaggregated enough to permit a listing of subproducts. However, some of the larger categories, such as cotton and jute manufactures, include subproducts that were simple and relatively homogeneous even late in the nineteenth century. Similarly, linseed, cottonseed, and rapeseed each represented several million dollars worth of LDC exports in the late nineteenth century but are combined under one heading, oilseeds, because of the lack of disaggregated data for earlier dates. It is likely, however, that each seed variety was in world trade by 1860, in which case conclusions about subsequent export diversification would not be affected. In any event, oilseeds is a common statistical grouping, so at least these procedures are not inconsistent with standard practice.

Cuba presented troublesome empirical problems because of a lack of itemized export data for several of the benchmark dates. Therefore, Cuban exports of sugar and tobacco are not included in the estimated values of trade in these products in the table. Although the trend in these numbers is probably not unduly altered by these omissions, the estimates at each bench-mark date are much too low. In 1900, for example, Cuba's sugar exports amounted to about $18 million, over 20% of the estimated value of LDC sugar exports. In that year the value of Cuba's exports of leaf tobacco were over one-third of the value listed in the table. Although it might be possible to construct estimates of Cuba's exports of these products at other dates, it is not necessary for the purposes of this work. The results are sufficiently strong so that it is unnecessary to resort to possibly tenuous estimating procedures for sugar and tobacco for other dates.

In the case of copper, however, I have used data on Cuba's exports of this substance in 1840 as a proxy for trade in the commodity before 1850. We know from other sources, including British import data, that Chile was exporting substantial amounts of copper by 1840. Unfortunately, I was unable to find an official record of the value of these exports, although the value of Chile's total exports was available. Since a record of copper exports was available for Cuba, I included it in the table to indicate that copper was established in trade before midcentury. However, the value of LDC exports of copper in 1840 must be substantially underestimated. Data for Chile were available for later years, therefore no other statistical problems arise from this source.

TABLE 3.1
Approximate Value of Less Developed Countries' Exports of Selected Products, 1840–1913 (millions of dollars)

Export	1840	1860	1880	1900	1913
Cocoa		2.1	2.9	17.0	84
Coffee	32.2	53.7	114.5	153.6	336
Copper	5.0	16.1	12.7	12.5	44
Cotton	11.6	35.8	96.9	107.7	300
Cotton manufactures		3.8	7.0	26.4	n.a.
Fertilizers[a]	.8	16.2	25.5	45.6	n.a.
Hemp		2.5	n.a.	13.0	n.a.
Hides and Skins	1.0	7.9	25.3	37.3	170
Indigo[b]	16.7	14.1	18.9	11.2	2
Jute		1.5	22.0	26.2	105
Jute manufactures		1.5	5.8	20.2	n.a.
Nuts		1.8	7.1	19.3	30
Oilseeds		7.7	29.5	42.6	220
Opium[c]	6.1	47.7	79.3	31.5	11
Rice	2.0	20.1	55.3	88.5	242
Rubber		2.0	8.5	73.1	210
Silk[d]	9.9	39.8	34.2	29.3	n.a.
Sugar[e]	49.0	75.5	99.8	85.0	132
Tea[d]	25.7	26.4	65.2	67.4	133
Tin	1.1	4.3	10.8	36.1	104
Tobacco leaf[e]	1.5	7.6	10.3	25.4	40
Wheat	4.5	3.0	16.5	13.7	n.a.
Total (a)[f]	167.1	391.1	748.8	982.6	2163
All LDC exports (b)[f]	238.0	543.2	1107.0	1529.7	3025
a/b	.70	.72	.68	.64	.72

Source: 1840–1900: Appendices B and D; 1913: C. Stover, "Tropical Exports," in Lewis (1970, p. 42).
[a] Guano + nitrate of soda + saltpeter.
[b] Includes small amounts of other dyes.
[c] 1840 trade was below normal level for the period.
[d] Excludes Japan.
[e] Excludes Cuba, Puerto Rico, and Hawaii.
[f] Excludes Japan, Cape of Good Hope, Argentina, Cuba, Puerto Rico, Hawaii, Haiti, and Santo Domingo in the years 1840–1900, and all but Haiti in 1913.

1900. It has seldom been asked, however, how important new goods were as earners of foreign exchange for the LDCs; conceivably, the appearance of new exports had little economic significance. The other assertion is that for all practical purposes the diversification of LDC exports began after 1850 and, if Lewis is correct, as late as the final quarter of the century.[6]

Before assessing the magnitude and timing of export diversification in the

[6] Lewis, "Export Stimulus."

LDCs, it is necessary to define the initial pattern of trade. To avoid being arbitrary in examining Table 3.1 let us look at the goods listed in the 1840 column, the 1860 column, and a third category (traditional goods) including only coffee, tea, sugar, opium, silk, indigo, and cotton. These products dominate the 1840 list and would be considered old by any standard.

As might be expected, the shorter the initial list of exports is, the greater is the decline in relative importance between 1840 and 1900. The share of traditional goods in total LDC exports falls 32 percentage points to 32%, whereas the share of all goods in the 1840 column falls 21 percentage points to 49%. However, the share of goods in the 1860 column falls only 8 percentage points to 64%, and a comparison of 1860 with 1913 shows no decline at all. Not surprisingly, pronounced changes in the relative importance of goods within the 1860 set took place, but the set itself retained most of its share in LDC trade until World War I. The implication is that the biggest changes in the commodity composition of LDC exports took place in the second and third quarters of the century, not later.

Existing commodity histories lend support to this conclusion. Brown and Turnbull write that Chile became an important copper producer in the 1830s.[7] Levin traces the beginning of the guano trade to about 1840, and Cheng shows that Burma began to export substantial amounts of rice at the same time.[8] Rubber and jute first appear in Table 3.1 in 1860, and, judging by the writings of Woodruff and Ahmed, they also were established in trade before then.[9] The beginning of the second half of the nineteenth century cannot be labeled a watershed in the history of LDC trade. The diversification process was a continuous one that had started at least 10 to 20 years earlier and, in some respects, was nearly completed by the date which many widely read histories adopt as a starting point.

Since Lewis holds that the three decades prior to World War I witnessed pronounced diversification in LDC exports, we also want to compare the 1880 and 1913 columns in Table 3.1. The share of the goods in the 1880 column actually shows an *increase* of 4 percentage points over the period despite the omission in the 1913 column of several goods from this list, such as fertilizer and wheat.[10] The rise apparently took place in the first part of

[7]N. Brown and C. Turnbull, *A Century of Copper* (London: Wilson & Co., 1916), p. 8.

[8]J. Levin, *The Export Economies* (Cambridge, Mass.: Harvard University Press, 1960); S. Cheng, *The Rice Industry of Burma* (Singapore: University of Malaya Press, 1968).

[9]W. Woodruff, *The Rise of the British Rubber Industry in the 19th Century* (Liverpool: Liverpool University, 1968); R. Ahmed, *The Progress of the Jute Industry and Trade, 1855– 1966* (Dacca: Central Jute Committee, 1966).

[10]Since Stover's estimates are not exactly comparable with mine, I have also used Yates to add the entry for copper and to adjust the totals for all LDC trade to include Chile, Uruguay, and several North African countries that Stover excluded because of his specific interest in the

the twentieth century, but it is enough to observe that by World War I, following more than 50 years of export diversification in the LDCs, only 16 products accounted for over 70% of aggregate LDC exports.

This finding is surprising because it indicates that fundamental change in the commodity composition of LDC exports proceeded rapidly when Great Britain was still the world's economic leader but slowed about the time the First Industrial Revolution ended and after modern economic growth spread to other parts of the world. The so-called Second Industrial Revolution and the diffusion of modern economic growth to regions other than Great Britain might have contributed to greater diversity in LDC exports by creating demands for new products and/or by fostering the introduction of new technologies directly into the LDCs. It is a mystery why the impact of these factors was minimal in the decades immediately preceding World War I.

Concentration of Less Developed Countries' Exports

Methods

The high degree of dependence on a few products for the bulk of export earnings in the typical LDC is today a matter of international concern. Tables 3.2 and 3.3 summarize the results of two separate statistical approaches to the question of how concentrated exports were in specific LDCs during the nineteenth century. One technique, the single-largest-product

---

tropical world. Yates unfortunately presents his data in such a way that it is impossible to fill in the other missing entries in the itemized list of LDC exports. China is omitted from Stover's estimate of all LDC trade, and here, too, it was not possible to adjust his figures to correspond to mine. Since China had a more diverse collection of exports than most LDCs had in the late nineteenth century, the omission of China probably biases the 1913 concentration estimates for the LDCs upward slightly. Using data for the year 1900, I recomputed the share of the 22 goods in total LDC exports excluding China from all relevant categories. The results were that goods listed in the 1840 column accounted for over 49% of total LDC exports and all 22 goods, 66%. These estimates are above those derived from data including China, as might be expected.

   Incidentally, the interpretation of these last two decades is complicated by the fact that several products suffered extremely severe price declines in world markets. Into this category fall sugar, tea, nitrate of soda, and cotton. In terms of constant dollars and in terms of the amount of LDC resources devoted to the production of these goods for export, there may not have been as large a decline in the importance of trade in these goods as the data imply. I explored this possibility by deflating the value of total LDC trade by the Imlah index of British import prices and the values in trade of eight well-established goods for which the necessary price data were conveniently available (coffee, copper, cotton, nitrate of soda, rice, silk, sugar, tea) by price relatives for 1880 and 1900 but found little difference in the results.

TABLE 3.2

Percentage of Total Exports Accounted for by Largest Product from Selected Countries, 1860–1900.

Country	1860	1900
Developed countries		
Austria-Hungary	14	10
Belgium	12	7
Denmark	51	42
France	21	6
Italy	39	26
United Kingdom	17	12
Canada	36	15
United States	61	18
Argentina	47	32
Cape of Good Hope	69	46
Less developed countries		
Brazil	53	60
British Guiana	73	54
Chile	63	66
Peru	50	33
Uruguay	50	27
British India	33	12
Ceylon	73	58
China	46	23
Dutch East Indies	37	29
Philippines	38	50
Siam	69	71
Algeria	17	32
Egypt	37	78
Mauritius	94	91
Reunion	90	56
Senegal	31	71
British West Indies	60	26
Costa Rica	85	55
French West Indies	84	61
San Salvador	83	81

Source: Appendix B.

method, is to calculate the share of the value of the total exports of a given country accounted for by the value of the single largest export. This calculation was made for the 20 LDCs and 10 now-developed countries for which adequate data were available in 1860 and 1900. The advantage of this approach is that it does not require much data from each country; the disadvantage is that potentially valuable data sometimes available for other products are automatically excluded from consideration.

TABLE 3.3
Hirschman Concentration Index for Selected Countries,
1860–1900[a]

Country	1860	1900
Developed countries		
Austria-Hungary	.31	.19
Belgium	.21	.15
France	.27	.17
Italy	.44	.29
United Kingdom	.25	.17
Canada	.40	.25
United States	.62	.32
Argentina	.49	.39
Cape of Good Hope	.69	.51
Less developed countries		
Brazil	.50	.64
British Guiana	.74	.64
Chile	.70	.70
Peru	.54	.50
Uruguay	.51	.43
British India	.41	.24
Ceylon	.74	.60
China	.56	.32
Dutch East Indies	.51	.35
Philippines	.49	.61
Siam	.70	.71
Egypt	.45	.79
Mauritius	.94	.91
Reunion	.90	.60

Source: Appendix B.
[a] The data in Appendix B have been slightly aggregated for convenience of
presentation, whereas the disaggregated data were used for these computations.
Thus, recomputation may yield slightly different results from these.

The second approach involves computing the Hirschman index (*HI*), a
formula that is sometimes used to reduce the full list of a nation's exports to
a single number representing the degree of export concentration.[11] The
formula for *HI* is:

$$HI = \left[\sum_{i=1}^{N} \left(\frac{X_i}{X} \right)^2 \right]^{\frac{1}{2}},$$

[11]See A. O. Hirschman, *National Power and the Structure of Foreign Trade* (Berkeley:
University of California Press, 1945); I. Kravis, "External Demand and Internal Supply Factors
in LDC Export Performance," *Banca Nazionale del Lavoro Quarterly Review* 23 (June 1970):
3–25.

where X_i is the value of the ith export and X is the total value of exports. A complete concentration of exports in one commodity would yield a value of 1.00, an equal division between two goods would yield a value of .71, and an equal division between three goods would yield a value of .58. The Hirschman index is also related to the coefficient of variation of the values of the items in a given list. Other things equal, the lower the coefficient of variation is, the lower HI will be. Varying inversely with the number of items and directly with the coefficient of variation are positive qualities for a concentration index. But a cautionary note must be sounded: The index gives only a rough cardinal measure of concentration. No index has yet been devised that overcomes the theoretical problems of measuring concentration when export proceeds are unequally distributed over a given collection of goods.[12]

Unless a high proportion of exports is broken down commodity by commodity, the Hirschman index (or any index) can give a misleading picture of the concentration of a country's exports.[13] For this reason the index was not computed unless at least 80% of the total value of a country's exports was broken down commodity by commodity. As might be expected, the number of countries meeting this strict requirement was smaller than the number meeting the data requirements of the single-largest-product approach. Nevertheless, it was possible to compute HI for 14 LDCs and 9 now-developed countries in 1860 and 1900.[14]

Finally, the commodity classifications used in constructing the basic reference tables should be discussed. Obviously, the higher the level of aggregation is, the more concentrated the exports of a given nation will appear on either the single-largest-product or HI computations. A disaggregated version of the modified Brussels classification used by Yates has been adopted here to avoid making the degree of export concentration in individual countries appear unduly high.[15] Nevertheless, a systematic bias remains in

[12]See the appendix to this chapter.

[13]See the appendix to this chapter.

[14]It should be noted that the samples represent nearly the complete populations of the developed and less developed countries that were in the network of world trade as far back as 1860. The main omissions from Tables 3.2 and 3.3 are the small countries of Tropical Africa that probably entered the world economy during the last quarter of the nineteenth century. These countries joined the network of trade so late that it is difficult to say anything useful about changes in their export structures over time. In addition, the data for these countries tend to be sketchy. Nevertheless, part of the impact of Tropical Africa's entrance into trade on the composition of overall LDC exports is implicitly captured in Table 3.1, which deals with commodities rather than with individual nations. The general conclusion is that as exporters of nuts and rubber, two comparatively "new" goods, the Tropical African countries contributed to the diversification of overall LDC exports.

[15]My classification scheme is roughly equivalent to the 3-digit Standard International Trade Classification and therefore is comparable to that used by one writer, Irving Kravis, on the modern period. See Kravis, "External Demand and Internal Supply Factors."

the data. Many of the commodities exported from the LDCs were standard and homogeneous throughout the nineteenth century, but the now-developed countries exported more highly differentiated products as the century wore on. For reporting purposes, these were often categorized under a general rubric, such as electrical equipment, that was impossible to break down into specific products. Although the biases introduced by these conventions may not be crucial for our purposes, they do make the exports of the now-developed countries appear more concentrated than they really were.

The Nineteenth Century

Means and medians were calculated for the 20 LDCs and 10 now-developed countries using the computations of what percentage of the total value of exports was accounted for by the single most important product in each country in 1860 and 1900. These are presented in Table 3.4. Among the LDCs, the typical country, as judged by the mean, earned 58% of its export proceeds from one product in 1860 and 52% in 1900. Comparison of medians at the two dates also indicates that little deconcentration of exports occurred.

Using HI one comes to the same conclusions. The relevant information for 9 developed and 14 less developed countries is set out in Table 3.5, which shows little change in levels of export concentration for the LDCs between 1860 and 1900. Not surprisingly, both tables indicate that the deconcentration of exports proceeded at a faster pace in now-developed countries than in less developed countries.[16]

The final two lines of Tables 3.4 and 3.5 show measures of dispersion in the data. The standard deviation and the coefficients of variation for the LDCs tend to rise between 1860 and 1900, indicating that the LDCs were becoming more dissimilar in their levels of export concentration despite the comparative steadiness of the average level. Several important LDCs, such as British India, China, and the Dutch East Indies, experienced substantial declines in export concentration, whereas several others, such as Brazil and Egypt, experienced increases. The LDCs showing large declines in export

[16]The t-statistic was employed to test whether the differences between the means of developed and less developed countries were significant at each date. Two-tailed tests were used. The difference between the means of Table 3.4 was significant at the .05 level for 1860 and at the .01 level for 1900. The differences between developed and less developed countries' means in Table 3.5 were significant at the .01 level in both 1860 and 1900.

It should also be noted that the persistent high concentration of LDC exports does not preclude the possibility of a country switching from one main export to another. This happened, for example, in Ceylon (coffee to tea) and Chile (copper to sodium nitrate) during the period in question.

TABLE 3.4

Percentage of Exports Accounted for by Largest Product by Groups of Countries in 1860 and 1900[a]

	1860			1900		
	(1)	(2)	(3)	(4)	(5)	(6)
	DCs	LDCs	(1)/(2)	DCs	LDCs	(4)/(5)
Mean	36	58	.62	22	52	.42
Median	39	62	.63	18	54	.32
Standard deviation	20	21	.95	14	21	.67
Coefficient of variation	.56	.36	1.56	.64	.40	1.60

Source: Table 3.2.
[a] DCs = developed countries.

TABLE 3.5
Values of Hirschman Concentration Index for Groups of Countries, 1860–1965[a]

	1860			1900			1952	1965
	(1)	(2)	(3)	(4)	(5)	(6)	(7)	(8)
	DCs	LDCs	(1)/(2)	DCs	LDCs	(4)/(5)	LDCs	LDCs
Mean	.41	.62	.66	.27	.58	.47	.57	.45
Median	.40	.56	.71	.25	.61	.41	.51	.39
Standard deviation	.16	.16	1.00	.11	.18	.61	.15	.14
Coefficient of variation	.39	.26	1.50	.41	.31	1.32	.26	.31

Source: Columns 1–6: Table 3.7; Columns 7–8; calculated from Kravis (1970, p. 25). Argentina excluded.
[a] DCs = developed countries.

concentration were large countries with a substantial resource endowment, although some small countries, such as Uruguay and Ceylon, also saw reduced concentration.[17]

The Twentieth Century

How do twentieth-century developments compare with earlier trends? Yates points out that in 1913, 22 underdeveloped countries covered in his study depended on one product for more than 50% of export proceeds and adds that by 1953 the number of LDCs from the same group of countries depending on one product for more than 50% of export proceeds had risen to 30.[18] Of the 49 LDCs for which adequate data were available to make the same calculations in 1900, 20 relied on one product for more than 50% of export proceeds. The upward trend in the number of LDCs depending on one product for more than half of export proceeds also suggests that conditions in this century have been unfavorable for the diversification and deconcentration of LDC exports.

The *HI* approach can also be extended into the twentieth century. Kravis has computed *HI*'s for twenty LDCs for the years 1952 and 1965.[19] The sample does not contain the same group of countries used in this study, although both samples have several countries in common. Kravis's level of commodity classification, however, resembles the one used in this study for earlier years. According to Table 3.5, the mean level of export concentration of 20 countries was .57 in 1952, only slightly lower than the .58 figure for 1900. The median level of concentration, however, shows a marked decline from .61 in 1900 to .51 in 1952. This evidence tends to counterbalance the fact that the number of LDCs relying on one product for more than half of export proceeds increased during the first half of the twentieth century. Nevertheless, the deconcentration of LDC exports between 1900 and 1952 hardly seems impressive. Although the pace of deconcentration apparently quickened after 1952, by 1965 the LDCs, by and large, still had not achieved the levels of concentration reached by the now-developed countries over half a century earlier.

Possible Interpretations

The extent of diversification in LDC exports after the opening-up period has been exaggerated in most previous studies. Although the number of

[17]A recent study found a surprisingly weak correlation between country size and concentration. See Nadim G. Khalaf, "Country Size and Trade Concentration," *Journal of Development Studies* 2 (Oct. 1974): 81–85.

[18]P. L. Yates, *Forty Years of Foreign Trade* (New York: Macmillan, 1959), p. 180.

[19]Kravis, "External Demand and Internal Supply Factors."

products exported by the LDCs increased, export earnings continued to be derived from a few well-established products, which suggests that structural change in LDC economies was not extensive before World War I. In the absence of other data pertaining to these economies, this conclusion must be considered tentative. But, as will be shown, other evidence about trade also points in this direction.

An explanation for the slight diversification of LDC exports after the opening-up period is called for, and it is useful to approach the data in terms of the Baldwin and Leff hypotheses described in Chapter 1. Because a full evaluation of these ideas and their relationship to the data would require a substantial effort, it will be possible to form only preliminary impressions here. But even a cursory analysis indicates that both hypotheses are helpful in understanding the historical relationship between foreign trade and economic diversification in the LDCs.

The Baldwin Hypothesis

Tables 3.6 and 3.7 classify 35 less developed countries or regions by their main exports during the nineteenth century. In Table 3.6 most of the exports that were *ever* significant in a country's export structure between 1840 and 1900 are listed; it is not implied that on any given date all were important. Table 3.7 is a rearrangement of these data in terms of the frequency with which certain critical commodities appeared among the exports of LDCs. The six goods listed (coffee, sugar, rubber, tea, rice, and cotton) also were among the largest exports in aggregate value by 1900, according to Table 3.1. Arranging the data thus, we can test the Baldwin hypothesis as a general explanation of persistent poverty in the Third World.

The most interesting feature of Table 3.7 is that the key commodities sugar and coffee have production functions with opposite implications for economic development. On the one hand, various writers, such as J. R. Mandle, have described some of the obstacles to economic development in economies based on sugar plantations. Broadly speaking, the paternalistic and hierarchical organization of society is the source of these problems. McGreevey, on the other hand, assigns the leading role in the onset of sustained economic growth in Colombia after about 1890 to increased coffee exports and argues on the basis of both theory and empirical evidence that the technology of coffee production is conducive to economic development. Leff's study of Brazil also implies that coffee technology helps development, whereas Kindleberger's argument that coffee technology hurts development seems dated.[20]

[20]C. P. Kindleberger, *Foreign Trade and the National Economy* (New Haven: Yale University Press, 1962).

TABLE 3.6
Selected Exports of Various Countries in the Nineteenth Century

Country	Export
Central America	
British Honduras	Dyewood
British West Indies	Sugar, coffee
Costa Rica	Coffee, bananas
Cuba	Sugar, coffee, tobacco
Danish West Indies	Sugar
French West Indies	Sugar
Guatemala	Coffee
Haiti	Coffee, dyewood
Honduras	Coffee
Mexico	Fibers, silver, copper, coffee, lead
Nicaragua	Coffee
Puerto Rico	Sugar, coffee
San Salvador	Coffee, indigo
South America	
Bolivia	Silver, tin, rubber
Brazil	Coffee, rubber, sugar, tobacco
British Guiana	Sugar
Chile	Copper, nitrate of soda
Colombia	Coffee, gold, tobacco
Ecuador	Cocoa
Peru	Guano, sugar, nitrate of soda
Uruguay	Hides, meat
Venezuela	Coffee, cocoa
Asia	
British India	Cotton, rice, tea, hides, skins, opium, jute, assorted seeds, silk, coffee, wheat, indigo, cotton manufactures, jute manufactures
Ceylon	Coffee, tea, plumbago
China	Tea, silk, cotton
Dutch East Indies	Sugar, coffee, tobacco
Indochina	Rice
Philippines	Sugar, hemp
Siam	Rice
Africa	
Algeria	Wine, breadstuffs, animals
Egypt	Cottonseed, cotton, wheat, sugar
Mauritius	Sugar
Reunion	Sugar
Tropical Africa	Nuts, rubber
Miscellaneous	
Hawaii	Sugar

Source: Appendix B.

TABLE 3.7
Countries That Export Coffee, Sugar, Rubber, Tea, Rice, or Cotton

Country	Coffee	Sugar	Rubber	Tea	Rice	Cotton
Central America						
British West Indies	X	X				
Central American Republics	X					
Cuba	X	X				
Danish West Indies		X				
French West Indies		X				
Haiti	X					
Mexico	X					
Puerto Rico	X	X				
South America						
Brazil	X	X	X			X
British Guiana		X				
Colombia	X					
Peru		X				
Venezuela	X					
Asia						
British India	X			X	X	X
Ceylon	X			X		
China				X		X
Dutch East Indies	X	X				
Indochina					X	
Philippines		X				
Siam					X	
Straits Settlements			X		X	
Africa						
Egypt		X				
Mauritius		X				
Reunion		X				
Senegal						
Tropical Africa			X			X
Miscellaneous						
Hawaii		X				

The nature of the production functions for other products is still a puzzle. Tea was produced by plantation methods in Ceylon and British India during the nineteenth century, and Lim's econometric analysis of tea production in Ceylon demonstrates that economies of scale exist for this commodity.[21] But it is not obvious that plantations hurt Ceylon's economic development in the nineteenth century.[22] Rubber, a plantation product today, was not one in the nineteenth century. If Wright is correct, economic retardation in the postbellum South cannot be explained simply by cotton technology, which is not to deny that the continued existence of plantations may have hindered southern recovery.

McGreevey argues that tobacco has a growth-inhibiting production technology and starts from this premise in explaining the failure of economic development to begin in Colombia during the period (1850s–1890s) when tobacco was that country's main export. Myint does not adopt the production function approach explicitly but observes that traditional methods of rice production are not conducive to development in peasant societies.[23] According to Baldwin, the technology of mineral production was uncongenial to economic development in Northern Rhodesia between 1920 and 1960.[24] This conclusion may apply to the nineteenth-century experience of such mineral-producing countries as Chile and Mexico, although mining technology has changed since then.

There are at least three observations to be made about Baldwin's export technology hypothesis on the basis of this evidence. First, several products, representing a large share of the foreign exchange earnings of the LDCs in the nineteenth century, had production functions that do not appear to have hurt economic development. Some countries, such as the Dutch East Indies, exported products with growth-inhibiting production functions and products without. Export technology can therefore be only one component of a larger explanation of why trade did so little to enhance prospects for economic development in the LDCs.

Second, if Brazil obtained only a few dynamic benefits from trade *despite* specialization in products that had technologies conducive to development, then export technology probably is not the key to explaining development failure in other LDCs. In other words, if a country exports a small share of its national product and/or experiences slow growth in exports, then

[21]Y. Lim, "Trade and Growth: The Case of Ceylon," *Economic Development and Cultural Change* 16 (Jan. 1968): 245–260.

[22]J. E. Craig, "Ceylon," in Lewis, ed., *Tropical Development*, pp. 221–249.

[23]H. Myint, "The Classical Theory of International Trade and the Underdeveloped Countries," *Economic Journal* 68 (June 1958): 317–337.

[24]R. Baldwin, *Economic Development and Export Growth: A Study of Northern Rhodesia: 1920–1960* (Berkeley: University of California Press, 1966).

whether the production functions of its key exports are good for development is of secondary importance, since export-led development will not occur anyway.

Finally, the emphasis placed on export technology, an internal factor, by some writers may reflect the belief that external demand for LDC products was strong during the nineteenth century. A central theme of this book is that the search for internal theories to explain the lack of response to the trade stimulus could easily stem from unwarranted assumptions about the inherent power of this stimulus. The export technology hypothesis might be a blind alley into which scholars have been led by misconceptions about other parameters.

The Leff Hypothesis

The application of the Leff hypothesis to the question of export diversification in the LDCs is simple and straightforward. The slower the growth of exports and/or the smaller the export sector, the less internal structural change would be associated with foreign trade. Export diversification, a probable and desirable consequence of structural change, would also be limited. The evidence presented in the previous chapter suggests that during the nineteenth century the LDCs did have either slow growth in per capita exports, a small export sector, or both.

Incidentally, developments in the twentieth century are not inconsistent with the Leff hypothesis. Between World War I and the Korean War rapid expansion in world and LDC trade was not the rule, but subsequently a substantial increase in the growth rate of trade and an apparent reversal of the modest trend toward more concentrated export structures in the LDCs ensued. The parallel between growth rates of LDC trade and the direction of change in the commodity composition of trade gives slight support to the idea that the Leff hypothesis could be applied to the entire Third World.

However, there are important nuances to the twentieth-century trade experience of the LDCs that the Leff hypothesis cannot explain. For example, the apparent reversal between about 1900 and World War I of the trend toward export diversification accompanied a boom in world and LDC trade. Also, Kravis maintains that the interventionist trade policies of governments in some LDCs in the twentieth century have helped throttle diversification, thereby keeping these countries from reaching their full export potential.[25] This, rather than the Leff hypothesis, may be the key to the poor diversification performance of the LDCs during much of this century. A full

---

[25] I. B. Kravis, "Trade as a Handmaiden of Growth: Similarities between the Nineteenth and Twentieth Centuries," *Economic Journal* 80 (Dec. 1970): 850–872.

analysis of the diversification performance of the LDCs in the twentieth century is beyond the scope of this work, but the possibility that the Leff hypothesis has a role to play in a full explanation of twentieth-century trends cannot be dismissed, these considerations to the contrary notwithstanding.

A Synthesis

Let us conclude this chapter by asking which LDCs were in a good position to reap substantial dynamic gains from trade during the nineteenth century. Combining the Baldwin and Leff viewpoints, we can list three conditions that must be fulfilled before trade can be expected to contribute significantly to a country's economic development: (1) a large export sector; (2) rapid export growth, especially in per capita terms; and (3) a comparative advantage in products with growth-promoting or at least not growth-retarding production functions. The evidence introduced in Chapter 2 indicates that few LDCs met even the first two of these conditions prior to 1900. Adding a third insures that few LDCs had any chance of achieving development through trade during most of the nineteenth century. Perhaps the only LDC in which all three conditions were met was Uruguay, the most economically successful LDC prior to World War I.

It should be remarked that although the Leff and Baldwin approaches are complementary, Leff was proposing an alternative to existing internal theories of the lack of response in the LDCs to the trade stimulus. Perhaps the main benefit of viewing the Leff and Baldwin approaches as substitutes for each other rather than as complements is that the Leff approach deemphasizes the idea that underdevelopment in the Third World is largely attributable to the machinations of foreign imperialists. No denigration of thoughtful leftist writers, such as Beckford, Levin, and Mandle, is intended. Still, by focusing on variables such as the size of the export sector and the rate of growth of per capita exports, which are not emotional issues, it becomes possible to entertain the simple but powerful idea that trade between the LDCs and the West did not lead to a serious start in development for the former before World War I simply because mutual interest in such trade was weaker than is often supposed.

Appendix: The Hirschman Index

In the special case where each product accounts for an equal share of total export proceeds, the Hirschman index does permit cardinal comparisons. For example, a country with total exports equally split among two goods would measure .71 on *HI*. Multiplying this result by .71 will give the value of *HI* for the case where exports are equally divided among eight goods, and so forth. Similar series can be generated if different initial distributions are specified. For example, squaring .58, the value of *HI* for three equal goods, gives .34, the value for nine equal goods, and so on.

When data are incomplete the Hirschman index can give a false picture of the degree of concentration of a country's exports. Assume, for example, that one product accounts for one-half of a country's export proceeds at a given point in time but that the values of other products are not known. If the Hirschman index is calculated on the basis of the single product, the value obtained would be .50. If the missing data consisted of one product also accounting for 50% of the country's exports, the value of *HI* should be .70. Since .70 is 40% larger than .50, the error involved in using only one product is quite large. Since the error is smaller with more data, I computed the percentage of total exports that were itemized by product for each country in the sample and averaged them by region. The results were as follows:

	1860	1900
Western Europe	93	93
North America	91	98
South America	91	94
Asia	90	89
Africa	88	96

A few manipulations of *HI* assuming 90% of the total value of exports is broken down by product should convince the reader that any biases that have been introduced by incomplete data must be very small indeed. Hirschman, in the work cited in the text, also gives theoretical reasons why his index is useful even in cases where data are incomplete.

4

Destinations of Less Developed Countries' Exports in the Victorian Era

Introduction

Most histories of the international economy in the nineteenth century hold that a "center" (ór "core") and a "periphery" existed. The center is usually defined as Great Britain plus the rest of Western Europe, although the United States is sometimes included. The periphery is the rest of the world, especially those regions distant from Western Europe. This characterization is warranted by even the most casual empiricism, but is it useful? Implicit in the center–periphery dichotomy is the idea that economic development in the several regions comprising the center followed the same path, with the result that differences in the impact of each of these regions on LDC trade and development were minimal. Whether there is any reason to assume homogeneity at the center is, however, open to question. Perhaps with the diffusion of modern economic growth from Great Britain the external stimuli to economic development in the LDCs took on new characteristics.

In appraising this idea, one wants a clearer picture of the destinations of LDC exports in the nineteenth century than is currently available. Table 4.1 contains estimates of the percentage of total exports shipped to various markets from Asia, South America, and two regions of Africa at four benchmark dates in the nineteenth century (1840, 1860, 1880, 1900). Estimates of growth rates of LDC exports to various regions between the benchmark dates are presented in Table 4.2. In addition, a description of the destinations of the principal products exported by each underdeveloped region is offered. A cross-classification by destination of each of a country's exports typically was not available or when available was not complete. However, if it is known that the total value of the exports of country A was absorbed by country B, then it is also known that each of country A's exports was absorbed by country B. Similarly, if it is known that country B and country C each took one-half of the value of country A's exports and that country A exported only one commodity, then it is also known that half of A's exports of that product went to B and half to C. This type of reasoning is pointless when a country's exports and trading partners are numerous. Nevertheless, the trading partners of particular LDCs were often so few in the nineteenth century and/or the export structures of particular LDCs so concentrated that reasonably accurate impressions of the destinations of specific exports from many LDCs can be obtained. Also, the necessary information is available for many of the British possessions, and cross-checking with commodity histories, other secondary sources and the import statistics of the consuming countries lends additional plausibility to the findings.[1]

An Aggregate View

Data

The geographic distribution of the combined exports of Asia, Africa, and South America at the four benchmark dates is shown in Table 4.1.[2] Since the data on which the table is based are tenuous in certain respects, a proper understanding and full appreciation of the results shown there are impossible without some preliminary discussion of the problems encountered in preparing the table. Herewith, then, the major limitations of the data and the strategies used in coping with them.

1. Central America is not included because the data for that region cover only a few countries and are available at fewer dates than data for other regions. The same is true to a lesser extent for Southern Africa.

2. The number of countries covered by the table differs from date to date. Membership in the network of world trade increased during this phase of the world economy's development, especially among the LDCs. The table

---

[1]Most of the relevant secondary studies have been cited in previous chapters.

[2]These data, of course, do not reflect perfectly the ultimate destinations of LDC exports because of the re-export trade. However, re-exports occupy a relatively small share in the exports of many countries; therefore the estimates based on LDC data probably do not err seriously. Also, the re-export trade tends to be self-canceling in the sense that a given country or region may be both a re-exporter and a recipient of re-exports of LDC products. A good deal of back-and-forth trade of this type took place between Great Britain and the European continent during the nineteenth century, for example.

TABLE 4.1
Approximate Geographic Distribution of Exports of Asia, Africa, and South America, 1840–1900 (percentage)

Region	1840		1860	1880	1900
United Kingdom	48	(44)	49	40	24
Other Western Europe	24	(22)	18	22	31
North America	8	(7)	8	12	15
Asia	15	(24)	20	18	21
Other	5	(4)	5	8	9

Source: Appendix C.

Note: Column totals may not equal 100 because of rounding. Figures in parentheses refer to opium adjustment described in text. The table does not treat Argentina, Cape of Good Hope, and Japan as LDCs.

describes the geographic distribution of the exports of the LDCs that actually were participating in world trade at each date.

Because of the expansion in country coverage, intertemporal comparisons of the geographic distribution of the LDC exports based on Table 4.1 could be misleading. There are two reasons for minimizing this possibility, however. First, data on the geographic distribution of exports for most of the major LDCs, such as British India, Brazil, and Egypt, exist as far back as 1840. Many of the countries for which 1840 data were unavailable, such as Ecuador and the Philippines, were small. Adding these countries at later dates does not greatly change the general picture.[3] Second, as will be shown, the trend for individual countries or regions often resembles the general pattern. Many LDCs exported the same or similar products; in consequence, they often were influenced by the same external forces.

3. A bias is introduced into the raw data by suppression of legal trade in opium between British India and China in the late 1830s and early 1840s. Indian exports of opium, which amounted to only $6 million in 1840, returned to normal levels after China lost the Opium War of 1842, forcing China to again permit importation of the drug. The effect of using data that do not reflect the opium trade is to make the Asian share of LDC trade in 1840 appear lower than it really was and to make the shares of other regions appear higher.

Fortunately, several secondary sources provide estimates of the value of the opium trade prior to Chinese efforts to halt it. Greenburg places Chinese consumption of opium in 1830–1831 at about $12 million and shows that imports of opium into China rose markedly during the 1830s.[4] Using Indian

[3]Chile is a potentially important exception to this statement. See Table 4.5.

[4]M. Greenberg, *British Trade and the Opening of China, 1800–42* (Cambridge: Cambridge University Press, 1951), pp. 220–221.

export statistics, Allen estimates the value of the trade in 1837, just prior to the Chinese crackdown, to have been $25 million.[5] The results of including an additional $19 million ($25 – $6 million) estimate of the value of the Indian–Chinese opium trade in our computations for 1840 are shown in parentheses in Table 4.1.

Destinations of Exports

Table 4.1 indicates a rise of five percentage points between 1840 and 1860 in the share of LDC exports being absorbed by the United Kingdom, if the estimates reflecting the opium adjustment are consulted. There is a subsequent decline in the British share, which accelerates in the last two decades of the century. The data further reveal a midcentury decline in the share of LDC exports absorbed by most of the other regions, with the prominent exception of North America, followed by a subsequent rise that is most pronounced in the case of Other Western Europe. Note, however, that the combined share of the United Kingdom and Other Western Europe falls from 67% in 1860 to 55% in 1900. It appears that even during its heyday the center was shrinking in relation to the rest of the world as a market for LDC products, whether the center is viewed as Western Europe as a whole or as the United Kingdom alone.

One might ask how the inclusion of Central America would affect these heterodox impressions. The fragmentary data that are available for that region suggest that in the mid-nineteenth century the share of exports from Central America absorbed by the United Kingdom was higher than for the other regions and that the share changed little until after 1860. But once the United Kingdom's share of Central American exports began to decline, it appears to have fallen faster for that region than for others. The shares given for the United Kingdom in the 1840 and 1860 columns of Table 4.1, in other words, are too low, and the shares in the 1880 and 1900 columns, too high. Nevertheless, if we assume that the British share of Central American trade did not decline between 1840 and 1860, the conclusion that a centralization of all LDC exports in Great Britain took place during that period still stands, as does the conclusion that a marked fall in Great Britain's share took place subsequently. The Central American data also reveal a more rapid increase in trade with North America than with other regions in the latter part of the century, which strengthens the conclusion that Western Europe as a whole took a shrinking proportion of the total exports from the LDCs.

It may also be conjectured how the picture would be changed if it were

[5]N. Allen, *The Opium Trade* (Boston: Milford House, 1953), p. 19.

possible to take account of British re-exports of LDC products. According to Imlah, between the 1840s and 1860s re-exports averaged about 12% of total imports annually; between the 1860s and early 1900s the figure was about 16%.[6] If these general figures also reflect the situation with respect to British imports from the LDCs and if the data on LDC exports to the United Kingdom were adjusted accordingly, the swing away from the United Kingdom after about 1860 would be even more pronounced than it is when unadjusted data are used. The proportion of re-exports in British imports from the LDCs may be different from the overall figure, but a presumption exists nevertheless that the conclusions would be strengthened if British re-exports could be incorporated into the computations.

Growth Rates of Less Developed Countries' Exports

The estimates in Table 4.1 imply that the rate of growth of LDC exports to the United Kingdom was lower after 1860 than the rate of growth of LDC exports to other parts of the world. The value of exports to the United Kingdom from Asia, Africa, and South America fell from over $375 million in 1880 to less than $300 million in 1900, whereas the value of exports from the LDCs to each of the other regions continued to rise. British import statistics record a similar decline.[7] Inferences made from value data can be misleading, however, because marked changes in world prices took place during the nineteenth century, especially after a severe price decline began in countries on the gold standard during the mid-1870s. It is unfortunate that appropriate export price indexes are not available to adjust the value of LDC exports to each market, but it is possible, using the Imlah index of British import prices, to approximate the real rates of growth of LDC exports at least to the British Isles and to other parts of the world during a large part of the nineteenth century.

The real rates of growth of LDC exports to the rest of the world, other than Great Britain, will be estimated using the following equation:

$$X = S_B B + S_R R,$$

X = annual average compound rate of growth of real LDC exports between year t and $t + 20$

---

[6] A. Imlah, *Economic Elements in the Pax Brittanica* (Cambridge, Mass.: Harvard University Press, 1958), pp. 206–207.

[7] Between 1880 and 1900 the value of British imports from the LDCs fell from nearly $460 million to less than $400 million, according to import data. Part of the difference in the absolute magnitudes is because these figures are c.i.f., whereas the ones in the text are f.o.b. Also, Central America is included in these import data.

B = annual average compound rate of growth of LDC exports to Great Britain between year t and $t + 20$

R = annual average compound rate of growth of LDC exports to the rest of the world between year t and $t + 20$

S_B = British share of LDC exports in year t

S_R = Rest-of-world share of LDC exports in year t

The equation indicates that the rate of growth of LDC exports is a weighted average of the rate of growth to each consuming region, with the weights being the initial shares of each region in LDC exports. With values given for X, B, S_B, and S_R, the equation can be solved for R.

Figures on the nominal values of total LDC exports, both including and excluding Central America, are given in Appendix A; figures on nominal values of LDC exports from Asia, Africa, and South America to the United Kingdom are given in Appendix C. These are based, unfortunately, on incomplete data, but British import statistics may be substituted, with the result that estimates of B based on them are consistent with estimates based on LDC export data. The shares of the United Kingdom and the rest of the world in the exports of Asia, Africa, and South America at several dates have been estimated in Table 4.1. Since these estimates also are based on incomplete data, there is room for error. But the difference between the United Kingdom and the rest of the world in the final results are so clear that it is hard to dismiss them by appealing to errors in S_B or S_R. The results of the procedure are shown in Columns 2, 4, and 6 of Table 4.2.

These estimates omit Central America. An attempt was made to use measured British imports from that region to rectify this deficiency. These *unadjusted* import data were pooled with the adjusted export data for Asia, Africa, and South America, and the computations were redone. The reason for not deflating in the case of Central America is that, as noted earlier, Eisner's index of Jamaica's export prices hardly changed during the second half of the nineteenth century. The results of this procedure are shown in Columns 1, 3, and 5 of Table 4.2.

Finally, the rates of growth of LDC exports to the rest of the world were estimated assuming that the rate of growth of British imports from the LDCs was a better estimate of the rate of growth of LDC exports to the United Kingdom than the rate estimated from LDC export data. The rate of growth of *total* LDC exports, which had been previously estimated from the export data, was retained for purposes of this computation. The results are shown in Line 4 of Table 4.2.

In Table 4.2 three trends stand out: (1) a fall to about 3% per year in the annual average growth rate of LDC exports between 1880 and 1900, after holding around or above 4% for 40 years; (2) a sharp and steady decline in

TABLE 4.2

Estimated Average Annual Compound Rates of Growth of Less Developed Countries' Exports to the United Kingdom and to the Rest of the World, 1840–1900 (percent per year)

	1840–1860		1860–1880		1880–1900	
	LDC[a]	AASA[b]	LDC	AASA	LDC	AASA
	(1)	(2)	(3)	(4)	(5)	(6)
LDC export data						
(1) Total	3.9	4.9	4.5	4.4	3.3	3.0
(2) United Kingdom	n.a.	5.4	2.7	3.2	–.2	.1
(3) Rest of the world	n.a.	4.5	6.3	5.5	5.4	4.9
United Kingdom						
(4) United Kingdom	n.a.	n.a.	2.7	3.0	.6	1.0
(5) Rest of the world	n.a.	n.a.	6.3	5.7	5.1	4.3

Source: See explanation in text, pp. 57–58.

[a] All LDCs.

[b] Asia, Africa, South America, excluding Argentina, Cape of Good Hope, and Japan.

the rate of growth of LDC exports to Great Britain after 1860 and especially between 1880 and 1900; and (3) a rise after 1860 in the rate of growth of LDC exports to the rest of the world, with a possible decline after about 1880. These trends are apparent in each set of estimates. The table also indicates that the rate of growth of LDC exports to the rest of the world was higher than the rate of growth of exports from only Asia, Africa, and South America to the rest of the world. As noted earlier in this chapter, the fragmentary evidence available for Central America indicates that an unusually rapid switch in exports away from the United Kingdom took place late in the nineteenth century; therefore, the higher estimate when Central America is taken into account is not surprising.

The most unusual thing about these estimates is the near stagnation of LDC exports to Great Britain in roughly the last quarter of the nineteenth century; indeed, per capita exports from the LDCs to the United Kingdom may have been falling.[8] British economic growth during this period, even allowing for the possibility of a climacteric in the British economy, was by no means negligible, and the average propensity to import in Great Britain rose from about .19 in 1860 to .25 in 1900 (see Chapter 6). Two general explanations are suggested. First, non-LDC suppliers may have made substantial inroads into the British market for traditional LDC products. Second, British demand for LDC products may have fallen or grown more slowly for purely microeconomic reasons, such as changes in tastes or relative prices. We shall return to these issues later.

The remaining sections of this chapter spell out some of the details of trade between individual underdeveloped regions and the rest of the world. The main reference tables on which these sections are based may be found in Appendix C.

Asia

Table 4.3 shows the geographic distribution of the exports of the Asian LDCs during the nineteenth century. The figures in parentheses are estimates based on the opium adjustment described earlier. The most notewor-

[8]Durand estimates world population as a whole to have been growing at about .5% per year between 1850 and 1900, and the population of several parts of the tropical world, such as Northern Africa and Latin America, to have been growing at rates over twice as high. However, the rate for the most populous region, Asia, was only .3% per year according to Durand's estimates. Comparison of these rates with the rates given in the final two columns of Table 4.2 suggests that the rate of growth of per capita exports to Great Britain between 1880 and 1900 was low at best. See J. Durand, "The Modern Expansion of World Population," *Proceedings of the American Philosophical Society* 110 (Nov. 1966): 136–159.

TABLE 4.3
*Approximate Geographic Distribution of the Exports of Asia, Excluding Japan,
1840–1900 (percentage)*

Region	1840	1860	1880	1900
United Kingdom	48 (42)	50	38	25
Other Western Europe	21 (18)	13	18	21
North America	7 (6)	5	8	10
Africa	3 (1)	1	2	4
Asia	21 (32)	30	29	37
(Excluding Japan)	21 (32)	30	28	28
Other	–	–	4	3

Source: Tables C–1 to C–4 in Appendix C.
Note: Column totals may not equal 100 because of rounding. Figures in parentheses refer to opium adjustment described in text.

thy trend is the swing toward and then away from the United Kingdom as the major market. Two important takers of Asian goods after 1860 were Other Western Europe and North America, and by 1900 Japan had become a large market for its neighbors.

A decline in the value of Asian (excluding Japanese) exports to the United Kingdom from approximately $215 million to approximately $166 million took place after 1880. Meanwhile, the value of exports from Asia to Other Western Europe, to North America, and to other Asian countries continued to rise.

It is also possible to make a rough estimate of the distribution of intra-Asian trade between 1860 and 1900. Table 4.4 shows the relative importance to six countries (Dutch East Indies, Ceylon, the Philippines, British India, the Straits Settlements, and China) of four regional or national markets (Japan; China and Hong Kong; the Straits Settlements, Malay Penin-

TABLE 4.4
Share of Various Receiving Regions in Intra-Asian Exports, 1860–1900 (percentage)

Country	1860	1880	1900
Japan	0	2	18
China	72	56	33
Straits Settlements	19	26	33
British India	9	15	16

Source: Same as Tables C–1 to C–4 in Appendix C.
Note: Column totals may not equal 100 because of rounding.

sula and nearby areas; British India, Ceylon and nearby areas) at three benchmark dates.

Although the underlying export data are fairly rough, the patterns in the table are consistent with prior expectations. Japan's share rose with its rise to economic prominence, whereas China's share declined with the gradual suppression of opium imports. Also, China probably experienced economic growth and development to a lesser extent than other parts of Asia and was less receptive to trade than other countries, with the result that its demand for imports grew more slowly in the long run. Singapore, one of the Straits Settlements, was a major entrepôt, but goods imported into Singapore were often intended for consumption nearby, not just for reexport to Europe. Similarly, many of the exports from Singapore were products of southeast Asia, not European manufactures. The rise of the Straits Settlements' share in the table therefore reflects not only this area's role as a way station but also its emergence as a commercial center in its own right.

The behavior of individual exports from Asia illustrates the general trends. In 1840 tea, silk, and indigo were the main Asian exports to the United Kingdom.[9] By 1860 the list had been sustantially extended, with cotton and to a lesser degree coffee and rice becoming significant. By 1880 rice, jute, seeds, and hides and skins had attained large values in the Asian–United Kingdom trade, although cotton and tea remained important. The period 1880–1900 saw stagnation in the value of trade in several previously important goods, such as tea, indigo, raw cotton, and oilseeds. Rubber and tin were the main export goods that showed rapid increases in trade at the end of the century.

Until 1880 the most important exports from Asia to Other Western Europe were sugar and coffee. These were shipped mainly from Java to Holland, from which they were distributed in Europe. By the final quarter of the century, however, goods from other parts of Asia were being exported to Other Western Europe in large quantities. Foremost among these were cotton and oilseeds, both of which were supplied by British India, but the list eventually came to include hides, skins, jute, and rice. The value of trade in some of the better-established goods, such as coffee and cotton, may well have fallen by 1900. Tin, an important good in the late-century Asia–United Kingdom trade, did not assume large values in the Asia–Other Western Europe trade.

The main export from Asia to North America until 1880 was tea, al-

---

[9] Interestingly, cotton had been an important export from British India in earlier years. Before 1820 Indian exports of cotton to Great Britain had exceeded those of the United States. See A. W. Silver, *Manchester Men and Indian Cotton* (Manchester: Manchester University Press, 1966).

though other goods gradually entered trade. These included silk, jute, and hides and skins. By the end of the century trade in jute manufactures and tin had commenced. In general, however, North America was not a large market for most of the goods produced in underdeveloped Asia.

The dominant good in the large intra-Asian trade throughout most of the nineteenth century was opium, which was shipped mainly from British India to China. Cotton became gradually more important, as did rice, which by 1900 had replaced opium as the leading good in intra-Asian trade. As noted earlier in this chapter, Japan was one of the largest markets for the exports of the Asian LDCs by 1900.

South America

Table 4.5, which resembles Tables 4.1 and 4.3, shows that after a swing toward the United Kingdom between 1840 and 1860, South American exports turned toward Other Western Europe and North America. Indeed, between 1880 and 1900 the value of exports from South America to the United Kingdom fell from $99 million to $68 million, whereas the value of South American exports to Other Western Europe and the United States continued to rise.

Only a few goods were exported from South America to the United Kingdom in 1840. The most important ones were sugar and copper, although the exact value of exports of this metal from Chile, the world's leading exporter, cannot be ascertained.[10] By 1860 a larger variety of goods was being shipped from South America to Great Britain, with sugar, fertilizer, and cotton making much headway. Until 1880 there were continued increases in trade in most goods *except* copper, but subsequently there was a decline in the value of trade in many goods, including coffee, sugar, copper, and fertilizer.

Coffee was the chief export from South America to Other Western Europe before 1880. Other exports were minor, although increases in exports of copper, wool, and hides from South America to Other Western Europe between 1840 and 1860 foreshadowed future events. By 1880, although coffee was still the leader, substantial quantities of several other goods, such as copper, fertilizer, hides, skins, and wheat, were being exported. Between 1880 and 1900 coffee and fertilizer exports to Other Western Europe continued to expand rapidly, and rubber became one of South America's exports to Other Western Europe. At no time in the nineteenth century did Other Western Europe buy much sugar from South America, while Great Britain bought large amounts until 1880 but less thereafter.

[10]N. Brown and C. Turnbull, *A Century of Copper* (London: Wilson & Co., 1916), p. 9.

TABLE 4.5
Approximate Geographic Distribution of South American Exports, Excluding Argentina, 1840–1900 (percentage)

Region	1840	1860	1880	1900
United Kingdom	47 (55)	52	41	19
Other Western Europe	35 (30)	17	25	40
North America	15 (13)	20	28	33
South America	–	6	4	6
Other	3 (2)	5	2	2

Source: Tables C–5 to C–8 in Appendix C.
Note: Column totals may not equal 100 because of rounding. Figures in parentheses refer to 1840 distribution on the assumption that all or nearly all of Chile's exports of $7 million was shipped to Great Britain, as is likely. This adjustment changes the impression of centralization in Great Britain between 1840 and 1860 to one of constancy or even slight decline for South America but alters the general impression for all LDCs (Table 4.1) only slightly.

South American exports to North America display much the same pattern as those to Other Western Europe. Coffee headed the list of exports to North America throughout the century, although several other products, such as rubber and sugar, became noteworthy.

Africa

Northern Africa

In the case of this region, Algeria and the Barbary States should be placed in one category and Egypt in another. Because of differences in the availability of data for these countries, combining them would obscure some of the fundamental trends. In Table 4.6, which pertains to Egypt, the pat-

TABLE 4.6
Geographic Distribution of Egyptian Exports, 1840–1900 (percentage)

Region	1840	1860	1880	1900
United Kingdom	17	59	67	55
Other Western Europe	46	25	15	26
Other Europe	35	15	18	11
North America	–	–	–	6
Asia	–	–	–	2

Source: Table C–9 in Appendix C.
Note: Column totals may not equal 100 because of rounding.

TABLE 4.7

Approximate Geographic Distribution of Exports of Algeria and Barbary States, 1840–1900 (percentage)

Region	1840	1880	1900
United Kingdom	51	23	7
Other Western Europe	22	67	84
Other Europe	27	3	2
Other	–	7	7

Source: Table C–9 in Appendix C.
Note: Column totals may not equal 100 because of rounding.

tern of an increasing share of exports to the United Kingdom and then a change of direction favoring Other Western Europe appears again. The shift was more belated for Egypt than for other LDCs, however, and by the end of the century had not proceeded as far. It is interesting to note that the patterns of change for Egyptian exports and American cotton exports in the late nineteenth century were similar. The percentages of United States cotton exports shipped to the United Kingdom in the late nineteenth century were 67 in 1860, 62 in 1880, and 47 in 1900.

In the case of Algeria and the Barbary States, the trend is also away from the United Kingdom and toward Other Western Europe. The data are somewhat unreliable because of French restrictions on Algeria's trade until the 1850s and, to one degree or another, at other times. But once Algeria was able to trade more freely, it did so to only a minor extent, as Table 4.7 implies. It is doubtful that any centralization of trade in Great Britain took place before 1860 because in that year over 80% of Algeria's trade headed to France.

Southern Africa

Before 1860 only three areas in Southern Africa were significantly involved in trade with the rest of the world—Cape of Good Hope and the sugar islands of Mauritius and Reunion. The first two shipped mainly to the United Kingdom and the third almost entirely to France, as it was obliged to do by French colonial policy. Table 4.8, therefore, traces the distribution of Southern African exports only from 1860, when the rest of this region began to enter the network of world trade and French colonial policy was less restrictive.

The figures in Table 4.8 show some surprising fluctuations (see last two lines of the 1880 column), but the downward trend of the United Kingdom as a market for the exports of tropical Africa is apparent, as is the end-of-

TABLE 4.8
*Approximate Geographic Distribution of the Exports of Southern Africa,
Excluding Cape of Good Hope, 1860–1900 (percentage)*

Region	1860	1880	1900
United Kingdom	35	27	18
Other Western Europe	52	29	50
Asia	n.a.	17	10
Other	13	27	22

Source: Tables C–11 to C–13 in Appendix C.
Note: Column totals may not equal 100 because of rounding.

century rise of Other Western Europe. Sub-Saharan Africa was the main object of the colonial aspirations of several Western European countries, but that region nevertheless experienced roughly the same pattern of diversification as regions that were in less political turmoil.

Central America

Data on the geographic distribution of exports of Central America are extremely sparse, making it impossible to calculate shares of exports going from this region to other regions at each benchmark date. But Table 4.9 shows the trend in exports from Jamaica during the nineteenth century, according to Eisner. The principal destination for Jamaica's exports by the end of the century was North America, and other regions were much less important.

Between 1840 and 1900 the value of the combined exports of Cuba and Puerto Rico to the United Kingdom fell from roughly $10 million to roughly

TABLE 4.9
Geographic Distribution of Jamaica's Exports, 1850–1910 (percentage)

Country	1850	1870	1890	1910
United Kingdom	78.1	77.7	32.7	18.7
United States	3.0	8.6	53.1	59.3
Canada	3.6	1.8	2.5	7.3
France	–	1.9	3.5	4.6
Germany	–	–	2.9	2.5
Other	15.3	10.0	5.3	7.6

Source: Eisner (1961, p. 270).

$4 million. Simultaneously, the value of exports from these countries to the United States rose from roughly $7 million to roughly $48 million. Fragmentary Mexican data suggest a similar pattern for that country.

Summary and Conclusions

Decomposing the world market for LDC products into its component parts leads to the conclusion that a modification of the traditional center–periphery view of the Victorian network of trade is in order. For one thing, the European center was shrinking in relative terms as a market for the products of Asia, Africa, and Latin America even during its alleged heyday in the second half of the nineteenth century, a conclusion that holds whether the center is defined only as Great Britain or as Western Europe as a whole. Also noteworthy is the apparent modest growth in British consumption of LDC products during the final two decades of the century. If the United States is included in the center, the picture changes and the center–periphery distinction can be maintained. Nonetheless, this evidence gives the impression of marked similarities and marked differences in the purchasing and consuming habits of distinct regions, including those comprising the center. The notion of a homogeneous center is therefore problematical.

The question, then, is what effect the growing pluralism in the world economy had on the external stimuli to development that were transmitted to the LDCs during the nineteenth century. Were changes in relative prices produced that encouraged the LDCs to produce commodities whose production functions did not enhance their prospects for development? Did the policies and practices of businessmen vis-à-vis the LDCs change as the external circle of contacts of the poor countries widened? What changes, if any, in LDC foreign exchange and trade policy were called for by the expanding circle of contacts? Although it would be difficult to address all of these questions in a book such as this, the next few chapters at least deal with several closely related matters.

Appendix

In order to ascertain roughly whether error in the sources might have influenced the conclusions above, I compared my results with existing ones for several other countries that are based on different sources. The works consulted were Adamson (1972, p. 217) for British Guiana; Fenichel and Huff (1971, pp. 34–35) for Burma; and Snodgrass (1966, pp. 367–369) for Ceylon. Burma is not separately covered in my study but provides an independent check of my results, as do the Eisner figures cited in Table 4.9. The results of the comparison for the percentage of exports going to the United Kingdom at several dates are as follows:

	c. 1860	c. 1880	c. 1900
Hanson			
British Guiana	92	68	48
Ceylon	76 (1870)	71 (1880)	61
Others			
British Guiana	91	65	47
Burma	65	n.a.	14
Ceylon	73 (1871)	59 (1881)	59

These results are consistent with the text, although some work is required to reconcile the 1880 results for Ceylon. Still, even in that case the long-term picture is similar, and Snodgrass acknowledges problems even with data as good as Ceylon's.

5

Determinants of Less Developed Countries' Exports, 1820–1860

Introduction

This chapter examines some of the relationships among acceleration in the growth of LDC exports in the first half of the nineteenth century, accompanying increases in the variety of products exported by the LDCs, and the rise of the United Kingdom as the largest market. The period 1820–1840, however, is treated more superficially than 1840–1860. Furthermore, the roles played by other developing countries, by reductions in transportation costs, and by liberalizations of commercial policy, especially the repeal of the Corn Laws, are only hinted at. Regarding policy, it is assumed that policies adopted by governments tended to be logical but perhaps tardy responses to fundamental changes in demand and supply and that for many products the immediate effects of policy are properly seen as lagged effects of previous changes in economic conditions.

The histories of trade in eight products (cotton, silk, rice, guano, copper, tea, coffee, sugar), which accounted for roughly 50% of the expansion in the exports of Asia, Africa, and Latin America between 1840 and 1860, are the focus of discussion, although several lesser goods are examined briefly. Geographically, the discussion pertains to most of Central America; to Brazil, British Guiana, Chile, and Peru in South America; to British India, Ceylon, Java, and the Philippines in Asia; and to Egypt, Mauritius, and Reunion in Africa. Few LDCs entering the network of world trade before 1860 are omitted. However, the exports of British India were more diverse than those of most LDCs, and several of India's most important exports— for example, oilseed, jute, opium, indigo—are mentioned only in passing. The main goods discussed account for at least 60% of the rest of LDC trade.

Some of the goods omitted in this chapter will be discussed later, but including them at this point would not alter the analysis significantly.

The analytical method is one of tracing common themes in the long-run behavior of supply and demand in particular markets. This market-by-market approach is to be contrasted with the general equilibrium approach, of which the intercontinental model developed by Mauro is a special case.[1] Ideally, we would rely on general equilibrium theory, but the limited resources available for this study dictated that we rely on partial equilibrium analysis.

Fortunately, general equilibrium analysis is not mandatory, since some of the assumptions of partial equilibrium analysis are fulfilled. Partial equilibrium analysis assumes that the object of scrutiny is a small part of the entire economic system and that the remaining parts of the system stay unchanged during the period of analysis. The former condition is almost certainly met in this instance. Exports from LDCs amounted to about 20% of world trade during the nineteenth century, and the share of world trade in world production rose from about 3% to 33% during the century preceding World War I, according to Kuznets.[2] Exports from LDCs, therefore, may have been 6.5% (20% × 33%) of world economic activity at the beginning of the twentieth century, while the figure for earlier years undoubtedly was much lower. The condition that the rest of the system stay unchanged is not satisfied, but account is taken of at least some of the ways in which the changing international economy impinged upon markets for LDC products and of the interrelations that developed among the various markets over time.

Ideally, a model of the world market for each product would be specified, and price elasticities of supply and demand, income elasticities of demand, and the quantitative impact of exogeneous developments that might produce shifts in supply and demand curves would be estimated using econometric methods. Limitations in the quantity and quality of the data rendered the rigorous specification and estimation of a model for each commodity market impossible given my particular resource constraints— and under any circumstances very difficult. But Wright's econometric analysis of the world cotton market eases this problem and sets the stage for subsequent analysis.[3] Wright finds that the price elasticity of British and American demand for cotton was low and the income elasticity high, from

[1]F. Mauro, "Towards an Intercontinental Model: European Overseas Expansion between 1500 and 1800," *Economic History Review*, 2d ser. 14 (1961): 1–17.

[2]S. Kuznets, "Level and Structure of Foreign Trade: Long-Term Trends," *Economic Development and Cultural Change* 15 (Jan. 1967): 7. See source for details.

[3]G. Wright, "An Econometric Study of Cotton Production and Trade, 1830–1860," *Review of Economics and Statistics* 53, no. 2 (May 1971): 111–120.

which he infers that increases in world income were the primary determinant of growth in cotton production and trade between 1830 and 1860. The world price of cotton fell, however, by about half between 1820 and 1860. Even a low price elasticity of world demand for cotton would permit supply factors to play a nontrivial role in the expansion of world consumption of this commodity during the first half of the nineteenth century. Wright nonetheless furnishes grounds for highlighting the role played by demand, and his conclusions probably can be applied to other products, especially natural fibers such as jute, hemp, and raw silk.

The argument in this chapter proceeds as follows. Great Britain became the largest market for the products exported by the LDCs largely because an unusually rapid expansion of demand for these products took place there in midcentury. Although the rapid growth of income and population in Great Britain after the Napoleonic Wars was the basis of the demand expansion, across-the-board increases in LDC exports to Great Britain awaited the appearance of supply bottlenecks and rising costs in the traditional sources of supply of such products as sugar, tea, coffee, and copper. It was not until established sources of supply became unable to meet expanding British demand at constant prices that alternative suppliers in other parts of the world began to feel the tug of British demand. Although economic expansion in other nations, including the United States, also influenced world markets for LDC products, the British economy was still the leading one, and the behavior of British demand was the chief determinant of the behavior of LDC exports.

Demand

Cotton

Although British demand for raw cotton during the first half of the nineteenth century expanded swiftly, the emergence of the United States as the world's leading producer caused the aggregate market share of the cotton-producing LDCs to decline. British India exported 87 million pounds of cotton to Great Britain in 1818, but not until the 1840s was this level exceeded. Indian exports of raw cotton to Great Britain averaged only 35–40 million pounds annually during the 1830s. Egypt, the other important LDC producer, fared better, increasing its exports of cotton from about 20 million pounds to about 35 million pounds between 1820 and 1845. The difference between the two countries can be explained in part by the good reputation of the long-stapled Egyptian variety and the poor reputation of the short-stapled Indian variety.

TABLE 5.1
Cotton Consumption of Selected Countries, 1826–1900
(five-year averages, thousands of quintals)

Period	United Kingdom	Rest of Europe	United States
1826/1830	962	542	175
1836/1840	1840	945	440
1846/1850	2584	1363	1091
1856/1860	4297	2846	1627
1866/1870	4417	2964	1732
1876/1880	5691	4657	3111
1886/1890	6989	7103	4599
1896/1900	7620	10,222	7119

Source: Sundbärg (1908, p. 286).

Industrialization gave rise to a massive expansion in cotton consumption on the continent of Europe and in the United States during the 1840s and 1850s. Although British consumption more than doubled between the late 1830s and late 1850s, consumption in the rest of Europe more than tripled and in the United States nearly quadrupled, with the result that in 1860 the combined consumption of these regions exceeded the United Kingdom's (see Table 5.1). Simultaneously, the United States began to fill its require- ments by consuming a greater proportion of its domestic production. Lon- don cotton prices, although fluctuating, rose from about 4 pence per pound for a standard grade to over 6 pence per pound between 1845 and 1860, a 50% increase when the general price level was roughly stable.

The surge in LDC cotton exports after about 1840 is thus correlated with rising prices and with heavier domestic use of American cotton. World demand outran the American capacity to increase supply to world markets, creating new export opportunities for other countries, especially British India. Silver reports:

From the twenties on, an intermittent demand for it [Indian cotton] developed in Lancashire itself where it was used to supplement a short American supply.... It was this occasional demand for Indian cotton as a substitute for the more expen- sive American which pushed up its price in Liverpool.... At the slightest indica- tion of any considerable rise in the price of American cotton sizable shipments were dispatched ... from Bombay.[4]

Egypt was also subject to American price leadership. Of Egyptian cotton, Owen writes that "its properties were not so unique as to allow it to avoid

[4]A. W. Silver, *Manchester Men and Indian Cotton* (Manchester: Manchester University Press, 1966), p. 38.

American price leadership, and throughout the period [1820–1860] it was subject to the predominant... influence of the larger American crop."[5] Although the competitiveness of Egyptian cotton improved before the 1860s because of Egyptian initiative, Egyptian cotton exports surely would have grown more slowly in the absence of an increase in the relative price of American cotton.

Great Britain sought diversification of its sources of supply during antebellum years. Various interested parties, including the government, sponsored efforts to increase production in other parts of the world, especially British India. The search for new suppliers intensified, as did British anxiety that regional conflicts in the United States would lead to a disruption of American production. Thus, superimposed on short-run price incentives was a desire by British cotton interests to diversify sources of supply in the long run. Conceivably, some additional LDC cotton was bought that would not have been purchased had current price been the only factor.

Silk

The story here is one of expanding demand in Great Britain, the main Western consumer of this export from China and British India. Average annual imports of raw silk nearly doubled between the early 1820s and early 1830s and tripled in the next three decades.[6] The annual average price of Tsatlee silk, a common variety, rose from 16 shillings per pound in 1828–1837 to 22.5 shillings in 1858–1866.[7] According to Cole and Deane, the main cause of growth in imports of raw silk during the 1820s was the removal of trade restrictions. But there were fundamental changes in the industry as well, which these authors describe:

> The second decade of the century saw a definite expansion in the industry stimulated by technological improvements, particularly in the throwing sections. . . . The proportion of raw silk [in total silk imports] which had been little more than half . . . in the mid-eighteenth century and about 70 percent in the boom of the early 1780s rose to between 85 percent and 90 percent at the end of the second decade of the 19th century. This was a consequence of the substantial growth of the English throwing industry.[8]

[5]See E. R. J. Owen, *Cotton and the Egyptian Economy, 1820–1914* (London: Oxford University Press, 1969), p. 162.

[6]W. A. Cole and P. Deane, *British Economic Growth, 1866–1959* (London: Cambridge University Press, 1962), p. 283.

[7]A. Sauerbeck, "The Prices of Commodities and the Precious Metals," *Journal of the Royal Statistical Society* 48 (Sept. 1886): 616–617. Much of the price data used in this study is taken from this source.

[8]Cole and Deane, *British Economic Growth*, p. 208.

To the price-reducing effects of processing advances must be added the expansionary effects of rapid growth in national income. The silk industry in particular felt the effects of rising income because manufactured silk, a luxury product, presumably had a high income elasticity of demand. Another reason why income growth was translated efficiently into direct demand for domestic silks and into derived demand for raw silk was that the British market was heavily protected. Many people thought Britain was unable to compete with France in the manufacture of silk, an opinion that was confirmed when the silk industry began to decline once the duty was removed in 1864.

Rice

The world rice trade was small in 1840, but soon afterward it began to grow rapidly in both value and volume (see Chapter 3). The expansion evidently was inspired by demand, since, as Table 5.2 shows, the Rangoon price of rice rose steadily until 1870. Another increase occurred after 1875. According to Cheng, Europe wanted rice as a cheap staple food, as starch for sizing textiles, as fodder for some animals, for brewing, and for mixing with wheat flour in making breads.[9] Great Britain, owner of the most advanced milling equipment, was the main European distributor.

In contrast to the typical LDC product, however, the best market for rice was not Europe. Most rice grown in Asia was exported to other parts of Asia or to countries with large Asian populations. For example, the British colonies of Ceylon and Mauritius received nearly half of the rice exported annually by British India, the top exporter. The coffee plantations of Ceylon and the sugar estates of Mauritius depended mainly on the labor of Indian immigrants. Thus, with increased British consumption of sugar and coffee and with the Crown's withdrawal of opposition to indentured immigration into British possessions, immigrants flocked to Ceylon and Mauritius and fueled the demand for rice in these areas.

Guano

Guano was the main fertilizer exported by the LDCs during the middle decades of the nineteenth century. Peru, owner of the biggest and best deposits, had encountered a resounding lack of enthusiasm in several marketing attempts that began in the 1820s, but between 1840 and 1841 the London price rose from nearly zero to £28 per ton. Guano quickly became essential to British agriculture, and British sea captains soon undertook a global search to find other sources of supply. Most of these expeditions

[9]S. Cheng, *The Rice Industry of Burma* (Singapore: University of Malaya Press, 1968), p. 8.

TABLE 5.2
Wholesale Price of Rice in Rangoon,
Selected Years, 1796–1900 (rupees per 100 baskets)

Year	Rupees
1796	3
1845	8
1855	45
1865	50
1870	70
1875	65
1880	85
1885	95
1890	95
1895	95
1900	95

Source: Cheng (1968, p. 73). Line 1 calculated from Cheng, p. 3.

failed, with the result that Great Britain eventually absorbed about 80% of Peru's annual guano exports.[10]

Behind the booming demand for fertilizer lay the increased intensiveness of British agriculture. During the first and second decades of the nineteenth century, the principal method of raising agricultural production was extending the margin of cultivation by consolidating or enclosing small separated parcels of land. The rate of enclosure was nearly 53,000 acres per year between 1802 and 1815, a period when it was necessary to expand output rapidly to meet war-stimulated demand. Although agriculture prospered during this period and its share in national income rose, by the 1830s the enclosure movement was on the wane. New types of ploughs were introduced, drainage was made more economical through the use of steam engines, mole ploughs, and tile-making machinery, and a greater variety of fertilizers began to be used. The famed prosperity of British agriculture between the 1840s and the 1870s evidences the value of the new techniques, especially since grain imports began to increase.[11]

Copper

Chile and Cuba were the leading exporters of copper during the first half of the nineteenth century. Chile rose to prominence during the 1830s, when,

[10]See J. Levin, *The Export Economies* (Cambridge, Mass.: Harvard University Press, 1960).

[11]See Cole and Deane, *British Economic Growth*, p. 160, and relevant portions of P. Deane, *The First Industrial Revolution* (London: Cambridge University Press, 1965).

TABLE 5.3
Annual Average Copper Output, United Kingdom and Chile,
1801–1870 (tons)

Period	United Kingdom	Chile
1801–1810	65,000	15,000
1811–1820	73,400	15,000
1821–1830	109,900	27,000
1831–1840	144,900	45,000
1841–1850	138,200	88,100
1851–1860	142,200	214,500
1861–1870	116,300	447,020

Source: Brown and Turnbull (1906, pp. 18–19).

according to Brown and Turnbull, "foreign ores began to be imported into the United Kingdom."[12] The country's production rose from an estimated 45,000 tons annually during the 1830s to 214,000 tons annually during the 1850s; Cuba's production rose from an estimated 9500 tons annually to an estimated 47,500 tons annually during the same period. Simultaneously, copper prices in Britain rose about 25% in real terms.

Demand for copper was greatest in the railroad industry, where the metal was used in building locomotives, and in the shipping industry, where it was used to cover hulls. The pace of expansion in these industries increased around 1830. In the years 1821–1825, 27 miles of railway were opened to traffic in the United Kingdom; in the years 1844–1846, the figure was 1084 miles. The peak year was 1847, when more than a quarter of a million men, or 2% of the occupied population, were engaged in constructing over 6000 miles of railway. Annual construction dropped rapidly thereafter but remained high by pre-1830 standards. The annual average value of shipping tonnage built between 1820 and 1829 was over £1.5 million; the figure was over £2 million for the period 1830–1839; it was nearly £3 million for 1840–1849 and over £5 million for 1850–1859.

Another reason for the increase in British consumption of foreign copper was the inability of the domestic industry to meet the rising demand at reasonable prices. Table 5.3 presents comparative data on output in Chile and the United Kingdom between 1801 and 1870. The table implies that after the 1830s Chile filled most of the new demand, whereas British output began to decline despite the rise in prices. According to Brown and Turnbull, the decline resulted from depletion of the best deposits.[13]

[12]N. Brown and C. Turnbull, *A Century of Copper* (London: Wilson & Co., 1916), p. 8.
[13]*Ibid.,* p. 13

Tea and Coffee

Detailed economic analyses of the behavior of tea and coffee markets in Britain during the nineteenth century do not exist, although several social histories are available.[14] An economic analysis of these markets is needed because tea and coffee were central in LDC trade and because the behavior of British consumption of these goods during the last half of the nineteenth century is puzzling. In an expansive age, total and per capita consumption of coffee actually fell. As a research problem the behavior of tea and coffee consumption in Great Britain during the nineteenth century has the twin virtues of being essential to any understanding of the evolution of the international economy and of being an interesting conundrum. What follows is a speculative analysis intended mainly to suggest research possibilities and working hypotheses.

During the early 1820s demand for tea grew rapidly in the United Kingdom, but a higher price rather than increased consumption was the chief result, perhaps because of monopolistic behavior by the East India Company, the target of much contemporary criticism. After allowing for changes in the general level of prices, the annual average price of a common grade of tea rose from 335 shillings per hundredweight in 1815–1819 to 394 shillings in 1820–1824, but annual per capita consumption of tea remained at 1.26 pounds. The price soon began to fall, and after termination of the East India Company's monopoly in 1833 and clearance of the company's stocks, the decline accelerated. In 1835–1839 the real price averaged 230 shillings per hundredweight, 40% below its level of the early 1820s. But per capita consumption was less than 15% higher. The real price of tea fell over 40% more during the next two decades, and per capita consumption doubled.

Per capita consumption of coffee in the United Kingdom rose more than threefold, from .40 pound to 1.25 pounds, between 1815–1819 and 1845–1849. The trend in real coffee prices was also upward, although sharp fluctuations occurred. In 1815–1819 the annual average real price of plantation coffee was about 80 shillings per hundredweight while in 1835–1839 it was about 100 shillings. Prospects for further increases in British demand seemed bright, and considerable sums were invested in new sources of supply in Ceylon. In stark contrast to tea consumption, per capita consumption of coffee began to fall in the early 1850s and by 1860–1864 was nearly 10% below its level of the late 1840s. With population growth, total consumption continued to rise, albeit more slowly than before.

How can the change in the relative levels of consumption of the two beverages be explained? A look at their relative prices is not illuminating because, as Table 5.4 shows, these ratios were highly stable between 1835–

[14]See, for example, J. M. Scott, *The Tea Story* (London: Heinemann, 1964).

TABLE 5.4
Nominal Prices of Coffee and Tea in the United Kingdom, 1815–1900
(shillings per hundredweight)

Period	Coffee	Tea	Tea/Coffee
1815–1819[a]	126	520	4.1
1820–1824	143	482	3.4
1825–1829	124	450	3.6
1830–1834	93	367	3.9
1835–1839	119	275	2.3
1838–1847[b]	75	175	2.3
1848–1857	54	129	2.4
1858–1866	74	168	2.3
1867–1877	87	160	1.8
1878–1885	78	120	1.5
1891–1900	95	80	.8

Source: 1815–1839, Tooke (1857, p. 414); 1838–1900, Sauerbeck (1886, pp. 596–697; 1901, pp. 97–98).
[a] Figures for 1815–1839 are 5-year averages.
[b] Figures for 1838–1900 are 10-year averages in most cases.
Note: These prices are not adjusted for changes in the general level of prices. In midcentury the British price level was roughly stable.

1839 and 1858–1866. Although a sharp fall in the relative price of tea did occur in the late 1830s, per capita coffee consumption continued to rise for another decade, which further invalidates any explanation based simply on changes in relative prices.

Another plausible hypothesis is that a change in tastes occurred, causing the British consumer's demand for tea to rise and the demand for coffee to fall. The opening of four new treaty ports in China after the Opium War of 1842, the debut of the clipper ship in international commerce, and especially the repeal of the Navigation Acts in 1849 stimulated domestic and international competition for the China trade. Tea was soon being carried to Great Britain in American bottoms, and races from the orient between China clippers attracted popular interest, making tea seem romantic. Crowds gathered on London docks or in Battery Park to hear sea chanties, and of the tea races, Scott writes, "The winning crew received as much as £500 in prize money. The first tea of the season sold highest, not only for its quality. People liked to drink and offer their guests tea carried by a famous ship. In a way, they thereby shared in its adventure."[15] Economists tend to be suspicious of sociological explanations of economic phenomena, even though changes in public tastes sometimes have serious economic repercussions. Yet it is not totally fanciful to think that the technological advance represented

[15]*Ibid.*, p. 146.

by the clipper ship itself and the clipper races from the Orient, the epitomization of the competitiveness of the age, so impressed the British public that consumption habits changed.

An amusing hypothesis is that the British brew inferior coffee, so that a substitute was desperately wanted. This interpretation is not persuasive, since what is required is proof not that British coffee lacked a pleasing taste but that the taste worsened after 1850. In the absence of evidence that British brewing skills declined at midcentury, this explanation collapses.

Let us express these speculations formally. It is suggested that the huge increase in British tea consumption between the 1840s and 1860s was not simply the result of a downward movement along a highly elastic demand curve. The argument is that the elasticity was low and that a marked rightward shift in the curve took place, an occurrence masked by the decline in the price of tea. Consider the diagram below. The British demand curve for tea may have approximated DD^*, which is stable and highly elastic, or DD_1, a less elastic curve that is shown shifting to DD_2. In the second case only bc of the total increase in consumption ac is due to the decline in price, and the rest, ab, is due to the shift in the curve.

The analysis is not yet complete, but the point is made. The alteration in the relative popularity of tea and coffee in Great Britain during a period when the relative prices of the two beverages hardly changed suggests that

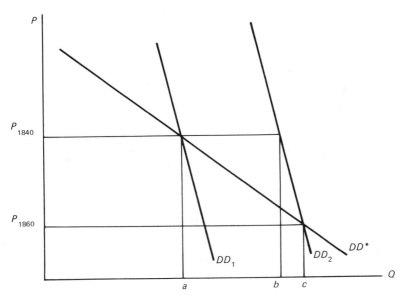

FIGURE 5.1. Hypothetical British demand curves for tea.

something besides price was operating on British tea consumption. Also, as noted, between the early 1820s and late 1830s, per capita consumption of tea in Britain rose only 15% despite a decline of 40% in the price of tea. The price decline during the next two decades, when per capita consumption rose 100%, was also 40%. This, to repeat, neither exhausts the theoretical possibilities nor implies that the British demand curve for tea in the 1840s and 1850s was highly inelastic. But a plausible case has at least been made that shifts in British demand curves for tea and coffee could be quite significant in explaining changes in British consumption habits in the mid-nineteenth century, notwithstanding the apparent predominance of supply forces as evidenced by declining prices. This conclusion, incidentally, is formally similar to that of Wright concerning cotton production and trade between 1830 and 1860.

Sugar

Per capita consumption and the real price of sugar in the United Kingdom were roughly constant between the early 1820s and early 1830s, indicating that increases in demand were not outrunning increases in supply. As the third column of Table 5.5 shows, however, sugar prices began to rise sharply in the mid-1830s; 10 years later they were over 25% higher in real terms. Predictably, a decline in per capita consumption accompanied the rise in price. But in the late 1840s, by which time the (real) sugar price had fallen back to the level of the 1820s, per capita consumption was over 25% higher than it had been in the earlier period. Clearly, the British consumer's demand for sugar had risen during the previous quarter century. Moreover,

TABLE 5.5

Per Capita Consumption and Price of Sugar in the United Kingdom, 1820–1859 (five-year averages)

Period	Pounds	Shillings per hundredweight	Deflated[a]
1820–1824	17.8	31.0	25.0
1825–1829	17.9	31.0	26.0
1830–1834	18.1	27.4	25.0
1835–1839	17.0	35.8	29.0
1840–1844	16.3	36.8	32.0
1845–1849	22.6	27.0	25.5
1850–1854	29.1	21.6	21.0
1855–1859	31.5	26.6	22.0

Source: For pounds, Mitchell and Deane (1962, p. 356); for shillings for 1820–1830, Tooke (1847, p. 414), and for 1830–1859, Eisner (1961, p. 244).

[a] Adjusted with Rousseaux index.

during the late 1850s per capita consumption continued to grow even though price was also rising.

The limited resources available for this study do not permit a complete analysis to be made of the sources of the expansion in demand for sugar. But it can hardly be coincidental that the rise in demand coincided with a sharp decline in the prices of the complementary goods tea and coffee that began in the 1830s and continued for over a decade. There are other parallels between the behavior of the sugar and tea markets later in the century, which will be described later. In any case, it is safe to say that many forces, including population growth, rising incomes, and declines in the prices of complementary goods, contributed to a surge in British demand for sugar in the mid-nineteenth century.

Other Goods

Table 5.6 shows the trend in the British prices of three other LDC products (tin, linseed, raw jute) for which the United Kingdom was the principal market. The value and volume of LDC exports of these commodities increased sharply between 1840 and 1860, and since prices increased for all of them, rising British demand is indicated. In the case of tin, there is evidence suggesting that the expansion of British tin imports was in part the result of bottlenecks in domestic production. According to Table 5.7, a faster growth of imports than of domestic production occurred between the 1850s and 1880s and accompanied the rising price of tin. This in turn implies that much of the rising domestic demand was being filled by foreign suppliers. In the case of linseed, rising exports from British India paralleled a stagnation of linseed exports from Germany. Linseed was one of Germany's most important exports before 1840, with a large share going to Great Britain. The rising price of linseed coupled with the stagnation of Germany's linseed

TABLE 5.6
British Prices, Selected Goods, 1828–1866 (ten-year averages)[a]

Period	Tin[b]	Linseed[c]	Jute[b]
1828–1837	64	40	n.a.
1838–1847	70	41	14
1848–1857	93	48	16
1858–1866	97	51	17

Source: Sauerbeck (1886, pp. 596–597).
[a] Adjusted with Rousseaux index. Unadjusted data also rise consistently.
[b] Pounds sterling per ton.
[c] Shillings per quarter ton.

TABLE 5.7
Production and Imports of Tin, United Kingdom, 1848–1885
(annual average, millions of hundredweights)

Period	Production	Imports
1848–1850	.12	.03
1859–1861	.14	.06
1872–1874	.20	.17
1883–1885	.18	.52

Source: Sauerbeck (1886, pp. 616–617).

exports suggests that this source of British supply was becoming economically less attractive.

Supply

Other things being equal, exports are stimulated by a reduction in their supply price. Exogenous forces that might cause such a reduction are technological advances, falling wage rates, and climatic improvements. Continuous rightward shifts of the short-run supply curve also can be produced endogenously, according to another elementary model. Profit opportunities in export industries that exceed those available in domestic industries will induce a shift of resources from the latter to the former, with the result that the supply of exports increases. The reallocation process may be augmented or facilitated by inflows of foreign capital or local reinvestment of profits earned from the sale of exports. It is not unusual for the superior profit opportunities that set this chain of events in motion to be produced by secular increases in foreign demand for the products a country or region is capable of exporting. An equivalent way to view the entire process is in terms of expansion of output along a stable, horizontal, long-run supply curve.

We want to know which model more accurately represents the experience of the LDCs during the nineteenth century. Conventional histories focusing on the post-1850 period typically adopt the model based on endogenous response to external demand. The canons of scholarship demand, however, that we look for important exogenous changes in supply during the early and mid-nineteenth century, a task that has barely been attempted in other general treatments. If few exogenous changes occurred on the supply side, it would be hard to assign to supply the initiatory role in the midcentury expansion in LDC exports and in the centralization of so much of this trade in Great Britain.

Any interpretation that stresses exogenous improvement in supply conditions must also show that the price elasticities of world demand curves for LDC products were not unusually low. Given inelastic demand curves, exogenous increases in supply would be reflected in price reductions more than in large increases in quantities traded, although volume increases would not necessarily be small. However, the rise in the prices of many primary products in Great Britain in the mid-nineteenth century is more consistent with the hypothesis that demand curves were shifting rapidly to the right than with the hypothesis that they were comparatively stable and highly elastic. As noted earlier in this chapter, Wright suggests that the elasticity of demand for raw cotton in Great Britain and the United States was indeed less than one and that, for this commodity at least, shifting demand curves led to the main changes in the world market.

Sugar

The sharp rise in sugar prices during the late 1830s and early 1840s was the result largely of rising costs in Jamaica, supplier of about 40% of Great Britain's sugar. Eisner writes:

> Exports of [Jamaican] sugar declined from about 1.4 million cwt. in 1830 to about half that quantity ten years later.... The decline after a brief span of prosperity was generally found to be due to widespread absenteeism resulting in poor management, antiquated techniques, and capital withdrawal.[16]

Eisner also observes that the abolition of the slave trade in 1808 and the emancipation of the slaves in 1838 hurt sugar production throughout the British Empire and that other areas eagerly capitalized on the problems faced by formerly dominant producers. The initial effect of emancipation was to limit the quantity of labor available in the sugar colonies, but the Crown soon withdrew its prohibition on indentured immigration, which allowed labor supplies to increase. Furthermore, tariffs were lowered in Great Britain during the 1840s, and the differential duties on sugar were removed in 1854, leading to further increases in the availability of sugar to British consumers. These policy changes were not really exogenous, however, since they represented a political response to the inability of traditional suppliers to satisfy expanding British demand at previous prices.

It is unlikely that technological change in the LDCs greatly affected the sugar trade. Manuals on sugar planting and cultivation were published and circulated during the 1820s, 1830s, and 1840s; the plough became useful

---

[16]G. Eisner, *Jamaica, 1830–1930: A Study in Economic Growth* (Manchester: Manchester University Press, 1961), pp. 246–247.

for cane hole digging in many places; new methods of fertilization were put into practice; steam power could be applied in certain phases of production; and the vacuum pan, which helped separate sugar from molasses after boiling, was introduced. But increases in output still depended on the availability of labor more than on new techniques, in part because in some LDCs new methods created more problems than they solved. Eisner describes the Jamaican situation:

> In a society lacking industrial skills the introduction of mechanical equipment was ... a hazardous undertaking; where a planter relied entirely on the new machinery he risked the loss of his whole crop if any breakdown could not be repaired locally. Mr. Price's estate was said to have got into financial difficulties as a result of his experiments.[17]

This assessment undoubtedly applies to other sugar-exporting LDCs, although prospects for successful innovation undoubtedly differed from place to place.

Coffee

There were few independent improvements in supply conditions in the chief coffee-producing LDCs when the main expansion in world trade began. As in the case of sugar, bottlenecks appeared in Jamaica during the second and third decades of the nineteenth century. After peaking at above 300,000 hundredweights in 1814, coffee exports began to decline, averaging only 106,000 hundredweights annually between 1836 and 1838. According to Eisner, the decline was caused by overextension of cultivation, poor agricultural techniques, and absenteeism. Emancipation of slaves created further problems, with the result that output continued to fall.[18]

Java's position also was slipping. Output there expanded from 7 million pounds in 1816 to 150 million pounds in 1840 in response to the secular increase in coffee prices, and in the process Java became the world's leading grower. But production shortly began to stabilize. In 1850 it was 100 million pounds; in 1855, 150 million pounds; and in 1860, 122 million pounds. Java's main problem was the inefficiency caused by the Culture System, a compulsory labor system imposed by the Dutch colonial government.[19]

Ceylon and Brazil benefited from the problems that beset Jamaica and

---

[17]Ibid.

[18]Ibid., p. 12.

[19]See J. S. Furnivall, *Netherlands India* (London: Cambridge University Press, 1939). The Culture System also applied to sugar, indigo, and other export crops, with similar effects.

Java. It was the lagged supply response of Ceylon and Brazil to the increase in real coffee prices in the 1820s and 1830s that helped drive prices lower in the 1840s and 1850s. Ceylon was admitted to the British market on equal terms with the West Indies in 1835, and in Eisner's words:

> Here rising prices, equal ranking with colonial coffee together with reduced supplies from the British West Indies provided a springboard for European investment. £3 million were invested in coffee planting in Ceylon during the late 1830s. In 1847 over 240,000 cwt.—about half of the imports into the United Kingdom—arrived from Ceylon.[20]

Additions to Brazilian production were larger than in any other coffee-producing country after 1840. Exports of coffee from the Rio area alone amounted to about 160 million pounds that year, and by 1860 they had more than doubled. Since little change took place in methods of cultivation, harvesting, and processing, output was increased by expanding inputs. Additional land was cleared from the still plentiful virgin forest, and over 370,000 slaves were imported into Brazil between 1840 and 1851, a period during which slave prices roughly doubled. The traditional technology, which contemporaries sometimes called "routinism," was criticized, however. "The soil," said one observer, "is cultivated with the methods and instruments of 300 years ago."[21] Nevertheless, as Stein remarks, "There existed no reason for radical changes in the techniques of producing coffee. A blind faith in ever continuing prosperity seemed to be the general feeling.... In the words of [one] observer, 'coffee pays for everything.' "[22]

Cotton

Supply conditions differed between British India and Egypt, the two main LDC producers, for Indian producers made no serious effort to compete with the United States. Indian cotton was the less desirable short-stapled variety; it was also adulterated at each stage of the journey from field to factory in order to increase the price received by the seller. Wastage ran 20–25%, as compared to 10% for American cotton.[23] The Crown, the East India Company, and other parties tried to raise the quality of Indian cotton; Silver's list reveals that in 40 of the 53 years between 1797 and 1850 attempts were made by a British subject to improve the Indian product.[24]

[20]Eisner, *Jamaica, 1830–1930*, p. 254.
[21]S. Stein, *Vassouras* (Cambridge, Mass.: Harvard University Press, 1957), p. 48.
[22]*Ibid.*
[23]Silver, *Manchester Men*, p. 294.
[24]*Ibid.*, pp. 295–300.

Foreign seed was transplanted into Indian soil, experiments to perfect a ginning machine suitable for Indian cotton were conducted, and special consultants were hired. Unfortunately, these efforts usually failed, and not until the 1860s did commercial exploitation of new strains of cotton become even remotely feasible in British India.

Egypt, on the other hand, forged ahead. Mehemet Ali, ruler from 1805 to 1847, undertook a program of forced economic development that made Egyptian cotton more competitive on world markets despite failing in other ways. Mehemet Ali's projects included reform of the previous land tenure system, encouragement of cotton planting, and enlargement and improvement of the harbor at Alexandria, which was also linked by canal with the Nile. "Instead [of development]," Issawi writes, "the country had landed on the road leading to an export-oriented economy."[25]

Other Goods

There were few major advances in the conditions of supply of other products that generated large amounts of foreign exchange for the LDCs. Guano was dug up by the Chinese and Indian coolies who had been brought in to work the deposits and was transferred loose into freight ships. Routinization of production brought the initial price down, but no other cost-reducing changes in supply conditions occurred. Methods of rice production also changed little during the nineteenth century. "Even today," Cheng remarks, "rice cultivation [in Asia] is carried on with basically the same centuries-old labour-intensive methods."[26] The same could be said of jute, oilseeds, and many other Asian agricultural exports.

China monopolized the tea trade during the first phases of the LDC trade expansion. Chinese methods were a closely guarded secret, but we know that plantation methods were not used. The very efficient plantation system of producing tea was not adopted anywhere until after midcentury and was never adopted in China. The sharp midcentury decline in the world price of tea stemmed from the removal of hindrances to trade (such as high British duties), from greater competition in the carrying and marketing phases, and from the forced opening of new Chinese ports to trade with the West.

In his study of Colombia, McGreevey treats the expansion of tobacco and other agricultural exports from the 1850s in terms of improvements in technique or reductions in costs of production, external demand factors, and advances in internal transportation.[27] He gives little credit to advances

[25]C. Issawi, "The Economic Development of Egypt, 1880–1960," *The Economic Development of the Middle East*, ed. C. Issawi (Chicago: University of Chicago Press, 1966), p. 362.

[26]Cheng, *Rice Industry of Burma*, p. xxiv.

[27]W. P. McGreevey, *An Economic History of Colombia, 1845–1930* (London: Cambridge University Press, 1971), chaps. 5, 6.

on the supply side; foreign demand is considered the main stimulant to trade. Better transportation is also regarded as significant, but from the domestic producer's viewpoint, this is as much a demand as a supply factor.

Rubber, a relatively new commodity to trade in 1860, is the perfect example of a product for which changes in supply conditions did not initiate the expansion in trade. Slaughter tapping of wild rubber trees, which destroyed the resource, was the main method of producing rubber in Brazil, the leading exporter. Not until the twentieth century were systematic plantation methods deployed, especially elsewhere in the world.

Summary and Conclusions

This review of trade in several of the most important products exported by the LDCs leads to various descriptive and analytical conclusions about the four decades between 1820 and 1860. First, the beginnings of the expansion in trade of the key goods appear to have been staggered. Coffee and silk were exported in great quantities from the LDCs during the 1820s, and trade in these goods grew without serious interruption thereafter. The main expansion in LDC exports of sugar and tea began slightly later and was less marked than in the cases of coffee and silk. Indian cotton grew less competitive in world markets between 1820 and 1840, although Egypt laid the groundwork for later emergence as a leading supplier of this commodity. Around 1840, however, expansion began to occur on many fronts. LDC cotton exports started to surge again; sugar and tea picked up their pace; coffee and silk continued their rapid expansion; and other goods, such as rice, copper, tin, linseed, and guano, became prominent in trade.

For most commodities the main market was the United Kingdom. A noteworthy exception is coffee, the bulk of which was purchased by Other Western Europe and North America. Other Western Europe also bought large amounts of sugar, and the United States bought significant amounts of tea. The contribution of these regions to the LDC trade expansion should not be underestimated. Nevertheless, Great Britain was not a minor market for coffee, for it absorbed most of the output of Ceylon and the British West Indies, and it was the largest market for sugar and tea.

A vast expansion in Great Britain of demand for many products the LDCs could produce clearly took place in midcentury, and it is this demand that seems to have been the most important stimulus to the expansion of LDC exports. The general explanation for increasing British demand is the rapid growth of population and income following the Napoleonic Wars. But sustained, across-the-board increases in LDC exports did not occur until several supply bottlenecks became apparent and substitution possibilities arose on a wide scale. By the 1830s Great Britain faced bottlenecks in its supplies of sugar, tea, coffee, copper, tin, and, to judge by German records, linseed. There also was a rising demand for cotton in the United States, as well as a spreading fear in Great Britain that the American cotton supply might be cut off. British agriculture was developing long-run inelasticities as possibilities for extension of the cultivative margin were exhausted. In short, demand pressure was building on the traditional sources of supply of a number of commodities, and large profits could be made by opportunistic people.

Naturally, the expansion of output and the entrance of new suppliers did not take place instantaneously. The expansion of LDC exports of some goods, such as tea and sugar, was therefore not contemporaneous with the initial surge in British demand. In some cases, there were other obstacles to trade, such as British commercial policy. But once the new situation was understood, rational political and commercial responses were made, stimulating LDC exports and causing them to flow increasingly toward the British Isles.

Exogenous developments on the supply side do not appear to have been critical to the midcentury expansion of LDC trade or to the apparent centralization of this trade in Great Britain. In most LDCs there were few important advances in supply; in some, there were obstacles to trade. China was hostile to international commerce; the Culture System contributed to Javan inefficiency; Brazilian coffee planters were often complacent; and the end of slavery in the British Empire led to reduced output in several colonies, although indentured immigration was an offsetting factor in the long run. New techniques were available for some types of production, but their dissemination was slow, in some cases because cultivators were not adaptable to new ways of doing things. The only LDC in which there were permanent and significant improvements in methods of production of export crops appears to have been Egypt.

6

Determinants of Less Developed Countries' Exports, 1860–1900

PART I

We have now arrived at what in most histories is considered to be the central era. But other writers neglect or at least slight the trends with which this chapter is concerned—the falling growth rate of LDC exports late in the nineteenth century, the United Kingdom's relative decline as a market for LDC products, the slow rate of diversification of LDC exports, and the possible connections among these events. As in the previous chapter, dominant themes will be highlighted, perhaps at the expense of some subtleties. The chief omission is the well-known decline in ocean freight rates accompanying the introduction of the steamship and other maritime innovations. But, as noted in Chapter 2, the rate of growth of exports from the LDCs was lower late in the century than in midcentury, which is hardly evidence for a low-transportation-cost hypothesis. Less expensive transportation was a partial offset to those factors that led to the decline in the first place.

The histories of trade in the leading products exported by the LDCs again will be examined as a way of addressing the main issues. The analysis of each market continues to be highly schematic. Changes in the conditions of supply for certain products within the industrializing countries that brought them into competition with the LDCs will be treated under the heading of demand for LDC products. Cost conditions in the LDCs will be treated under the heading of supply, although it could be argued that the competitive position of non-LDCs should be treated under this heading as well.

Before embarking on the main discussion, however, it is necessary to digress briefly on the international implications of the so-called Great Depression between 1873 and 1896 and to run a statistical test of the relative importance of external demand versus internal supply in shaping trends in LDC trade after 1860.

The Great Depression

It is widely held that a long retardation in economic growth took place in the world economy between the mid-1870s and mid-1890s, a period when prices and nominal interest rates plunged in many countries, and some historians have seized on this retardation, or Great Depression, to explain the simultaneous decline in the growth rate of world trade. Lending plausibility to this interpretation is the rapid growth of trade after business conditions began to improve in 1896. The synchronization of business cycles and trade cycles is a strong argument in favor of retardation in the growth of world income as a cause of the late-nineteenth-century fall in the growth rate of LDC trade.

There are, nonetheless, several objections to this interpretation. First, scholars do not agree that a Great Depression occurred in any real sense despite the secular decline in prices and nominal interest rates. The relevant arguments against the existence of a Great Depression are summarized by Good, who finds no evidence of secular retardation in Austrian economic growth over the period in question.[1] McCloskey holds that the "climacteric" in British growth in the late nineteenth century is a fantasy.[2] He also observes that Great Britain did not compare badly with the United States and Germany in terms of economic performance.[3] Saul labels the Great Depression a "myth."[4] On the other hand, Williamson, citing declines in real interest rates, claims that the United States and other industrial countries did experience a retardation of growth between the 1870s and 1890s.[5] With the existence of the Great Depression in dispute, an opportunity is available to provide an alternative explanation for fluctuations in the growth rates of world and LDC trade.

Second, an explanation of fluctuations in the rate of growth of international trade based on a slowing of the growth of *world* income implies, by itself, that the geographic composition of LDC exports would not have

[1]D. F. Good, "Stagnation and Take-Off in Austria, 1873–1913," *Economic History Review*, 2d ser. 27 (Feb. 1974): 72–87.

[2]D. McCloskey, "Did Victorian Britain Fail?," *ibid.* 23 (Dec. 1970): 446–459.

[3]D. McCloskey, "Victorian Growth: A Rejoinder," *ibid.* 27 (May 1974): 275–277.

[4]S. B. Saul, *The Myth of the Great Depression, 1873–1896* (London: Macmillan, 1969).

[5]J. G. Williamson, "Late Nineteenth-Century American Retardation: A Neoclassical Analysis," *Journal of Economic History* 33 (Sept. 1973): 581–607.

changed. In fact, marked diversification took place in the trading partners of Asian, African, and Latin American countries, with the importance of Great Britain falling. Even with the most pessimistic view of the British economy, it is hard to explain near stagnation of British demand for LDC products simply in terms of retardation in Great Britain's growth rate.

This argument is backed by the behavior of the imports–national-product ratio in the main industrializing countries. As Table 6.1 shows, the increase of six percentage points in the British import proportion between 1860 and 1900 was greater than the increase in any other country. The ratio of imports to national product in the United States actually fell; following an initial increase, the ratios also slipped back in Germany and France. These are averages that conceal developments in demand for specific LDC products, but they still indicate that the geographic diversification of LDC exports was not merely the result of a relative slowing in the rate of economic growth in the United Kingdom, or of a fall in the proportion of aggregate demand reflected in imports.

Third, the work of Kuznets cited in Chapter 2 indicates that over the century or so preceding World War I world trade grew faster than world income. Although growth in world income obviously influenced the long-term growth rate of world trade, trade grew faster than income, implying that basic structural forces also were operating. It is unlikely that these forces stopped working during the Great Depression, although their channels of influence have yet to be articulated.

Finally, theoretical reasons exist why fluctuations in the growth rate of world trade need not result exclusively from fluctuations in the growth rate of world income. Assume that the decline in the growth rate of world demand for LDC products was the main cause of the fall in the growth rate of LDC exports. Also assume that the decline in the growth rate of world demand was not the result of a long-swing retardation in world economic

TABLE 6.1
Import Proportions for Selected Countries, 1860–1900

Period	United Kingdom	Germany	France	United States
c. 1860	.19	.15	.10	.07
c. 1870	.21	.22	.16	.07
c. 1880	.25	.17	.18	.06
c. 1890	.25	.17	.16	.06
c. 1900	.25	.19	.14	.04

Source: Kuznets (1967).

growth per se but was the result of some as yet unspecified structural change. Under these conditions and in the absence of substantial inflows of capital, increased earnings from invisible exports, and improvements in the terms of trade, merchandise imports into the LDCs could not have grown more rapidly than merchandise exports for long. Therefore, the slackening in world demand for LDC exports would have been accompanied by a slackening of LDC demand for imports from the rest of the world. Since imports into and exports from the LDCs amounted to roughly 35–40% of world trade during the nineteenth century, an explanation of slowing growth in LDC trade based on structural change can explain much of the fall in the growth rate of world trade as well.

In sum, the Great Depression may have a role to play in a complete explanation of events, but it is unlikely that it tells the whole story or that microeconomic influences on the propensities of countries to engage in international commerce can safely be ignored.

External Demand versus Internal Supply: A Test

The idea of complementary trade underlies most interpretations of trade between the LDCs and the rest of the world during the second half of the nineteenth century. It is argued that rapidly expanding demand for primary products at the industrial center of the world economy played the primary role in shaping long-term economic and political relations between the LDCs and the advanced nations. Although casual empiricism suggests many instances of complementary relationships, casual observation also suggests instances of substitution between goods produced in the LDCs on one hand and the industrializing nations on the other. Obvious examples are synthetic and natural dyes, as well as European beet sugar and tropical cane sugar. It is natural to ask whether for a given LDC the positive impact on exports of rising world income and population was offset (or enhanced) by the appearance (or disappearance) of substitutes for the country's traditional products. In short, the question is whether late Victorian trends in LDC exports should be seen as the net result of interplay among many variables and not just as a consequence of new demands emerging at the industrial center of the world economy after the Industrial Revolution.

Existing histories usually assume that exogenous increases in the supply of exports from the LDCs had little, if any, significance in the overall picture. Before the third quarter of the century shifts of this sort probably had small importance, but with the increased integration of the network of world trade and larger international flows of technology in later years, supply shifts could have played a larger role.

The problem of how to evaluate the contributions of internal supply and external demand to LDC export performance has been addressed in several studies of international trade in the twentieth century. One technique employed by Kravis and others analyzes the export performance of a country in terms of four factors: (1) a world market factor; (2) a competitiveness factor; (3) a diversification factor; and (4) an "own performance" variable.[6] The first of these is a demand proxy, and the other three are supply proxies.

The world market variable is an index-number comparison of the country's actual exports at the initial date and what the exports *would have been* at the terminal date if the country had maintained its share in world trade for each of its traditional exports. The competitiveness factor is a comparison of the value of the country's exports in the initial period and the hypothetical value in the terminal period if the value of world trade in each of the country's traditional exports stayed constant and the country's share in trade in each product had been allowed to change as it in fact did. The diversification factor is a ratio of the share of traditional products in exports at the initial date to the share of the same products at the terminal date. The "own performance" variable is computed by multiplying the two preceding variables. It summarizes net change on all supply fronts.

Previous studies using this approach have been based on data covering only 10 to 20 years in the postwar period, but here data covering 40 years (1860–1900) are used. It is reasonable to assume that short-term influences, cyclical or otherwise, will counterbalance each other and that the secular determinants of LDC export performance will be more apparent if the period of analysis is long.

Methodological Remarks

In Table 6.2 the relevant calculations on export performance pertaining to 12 LDCs are displayed for two benchmark dates, 1860 and 1900. Because gaps existed in the data, extreme care was taken in admitting countries into the sample, which explains why the list is so short. Two criteria were used: (1) the extent to which reasonably good estimates of the value of world trade in given LDC exports were available for the two benchmark dates (see Appendix D); and (2) the degree to which a detailed and complete itemization of a country's exports by product was available.

Although imperfections existed in the data and although these had to be

[6]See I. Kravis, "External Demand and Internal Supply Factors in LDC Export Performance," *Banca Nazionale del Lavoro Quarterly Review* 23 (June 1970): 3–25, and works cited therein.

TABLE 6.2
Export Performance of Selected Less Developed Countries, 1860–1900

Country	(1) Total export earnings	(2) World market factor	(3) Competitive factor	(4) Diversification factor	(5) "Own performance" indicator
Egypt	506	151	340	100	340
Costa Rica	413	277	100	185	185
Siam	391	346	68	100	68
Brazil	326	383	94	100	94
Philippines	286	233	97	120	118
Ceylon	274	227	18	1250	225
Dutch East Indies	273	311	63	172	108
British India	260	210	91	113	103
San Salvador	161	239	17	528	90
British Guiana	135	243	68	139	95
French West Indies	95	283	48	100	48
Mauritius	92	288	34	100	34

Source: Appendices B and D; see also Hanson (1977).
Note: Philippines and Siamese actual export performance calculated on 1864–1904 basis. Egypt and Dutch East Indies actual export performance calculated on 1859–1899. Brazil calculated on 1861–1901. British Guiana diversification calculated from Adamson (1972, p. 215).

dealt with somewhat arbitrarily, it is remarkable how well the arrangement of the countries in Table 6.2 in terms of the world market, the competitiveness, and the other factors dovetails with expectations based on well-known history. The sugar economies of British Guiana, French West Indies, and Mauritius, for example, show similar values for the world market factor and rank low on the competitiveness index. It is not surprising to see Egypt ranked low on the world market scale but high on the competitiveness index, since Egypt managed to improve its competitive position vis-à-vis the rest of the world despite lagging world demand for cotton. The abysmal ranking of Ceylon on the competitiveness index and its high ranking on the diversification index follow from the fact that Ceylon's coffee industry was devastated by a coffee bush disease during and after the 1870s, leading to collapse of the industry and to an assiduous search for new exports by landowners.

Incidentally, although the sample of countries is small, it is representative. Both large and small countries are included. Highly diversified exporters (e.g., Dutch East Indies) and highly concentrated exporters (e.g., Mauritius) are present. Collectively, the sample countries represent about 60% of LDC exports in 1900. It may be objected that the sample is biased toward countries that specialized in sugar, thereby slanting the results in favor of the hypotheses under examination. To meet this objection, the French West Indies and Mauritius were removed from the sample, and the rank correlations reported in the following section were redone. The results are much the same as those obtained using the larger sample, although statistical significance levels tend to be lower.

It should be noted that for five countries the diversification index is placed at 100, indicating no diversification. Actually, this should be interpreted to mean negligible or small change, since diversification may not be measured precisely given the flaws in the underlying data. The impression of negligible diversification was reinforced by a reading of various secondary studies.

Results

If world market expansion were the overriding influence on LDC exports, a high and positive correlation ought to exist between the ranks of the countries with respect to actual export performance and the ranks with respect to the world market factor. If supply conditions were important, the rank correlation between actual export performance and one or more of the three supply proxies should be high and positive. The Spearman coefficients of rank correlation (with significance levels in parentheses) between the index of actual export earnings and each of the other factors are:

Factor	12 countries	10 countries
World market	−.09 (>.40)	.07 (>.40)
Competitiveness	.72 (.01)	.71 (.05)
Diversification	.01 (>.40)	−.43 (.20)
"Own performance"	.65 (.05)	.39 (.20)

The coefficient of rank correlation between export earnings and the world market factor is negative for the 12-country sample and barely positive for the 10-country sample, although the coefficient is not significant at a very high level in either case. Except for the 10-country diversification index, the rank correlations between export performance and the other factors are positive. In the cases of the competitiveness and "own performance" indicators they are also high and, except in one instance, are significant at least at the 5% confidence level. These results are similar to those reported by Kravis, except that the diversification variable does not perform well here.

In the broadest sense, these statistical results indicate the variety of channels through which modern economic growth affected economic relations among different parts of the world during the nineteenth century. Although expanding markets cannot be ignored, it was not, as the conventional literature would lead one to believe, simply a matter of expanding demand at the center drawing primary products out of the periphery. In fact, world demand conditions differed markedly from one LDC to another, as Column 2 of Table 6.2 suggests. The competitive situation was also extremely important, perhaps more so than demand. Clearly, further refinement of existing portrayals of the nineteenth-century world economic order is called for, although the findings here are suggestive at best. Marxists and radicals, however, might consider qualifying the assertion that the now-developed countries were "rapacious" (to use a current cliché) during this phase of their development in light of the evidence of intense competition between LDCs and non-LDCs in various lines of production.

PART II

In Part I of this chapter a theme was introduced that is not explored in other histories of the evolution of the international economy during the late nineteenth century—that LDC trade patterns were not shaped strictly by rising demand for commodities in the West but were also affected by the emergence of industries in the West that posed a direct threat to the LDCs. Furthermore, how the LDCs reacted to the challenge was an important

determinant of the rapidity with which their exports expanded. The following review of market conditions for LDC products reveals that in only a few
markets—notably those for rubber and tin—was the pattern essentially one
of robust demand-dominated expansion during the late nineteenth century.
In fact, a slowing in the growth of British demand for some LDC products
had a great impact on LDC exports. With British demand starting to flag
and other developing regions initiating a wide-ranging competition with the
LDCs, it is not surprising that the rate of growth of LDC exports fell late in
the nineteenth century.

Demand

Cotton

The four decades between 1860 and 1900 were ones of irregular growth
in LDC cotton exports. The value of tropical exports of raw cotton grew
from $33 million to $97 million between 1860 and 1880 but only $11
million more between 1880 and 1900. Meanwhile, the geographic distribution of LDC cotton exports changed drastically. The main export markets
for cotton produced in British India are shown in Table 6.3. The value of
exports from British India to the United Kingdom increased between 1860
and 1880 but by 1900 had become negligible. Exports of cotton from
India to continental Europe grew rapidly between 1860 and 1880 but
plummeted at the end of the century. By 1900 most of British India's cotton
exports were being shipped to Japan. Exports of Egyptian cotton, however,
showed rapid growth to all European markets after 1860, although growth
slowed near the end of the century.

The disruption of production in the United States during and immediately
after the Civil War altered trends in LDC cotton exports until about 1880.
Eventually, however, the United States regained its preeminent position in
cotton production, which contributed to the decline in the rate of growth of
LDC cotton exports during the last quarter of the century. Egypt, though,
benefited from improved domestic productivity, as will be shown.

For further analysis of the world cotton market during the late nineteenth
century let us turn to Wright.[7] He points out that a critical development in
the world cotton market after about 1860 was a decline in the growth rate
of world demand. He does not pretend to know why British demand in
particular grew so slowly, but offers the following thoughts, which are also

[7]See G. Wright, "Cotton Competition and the Post-Bellum Recovery of the American
South," *Journal of Economic History* 34 (Sept. 1974): 610–635.

TABLE 6.3
Destinations of Raw Cotton Exports from British India, 1860–1900 (millions of dollars)

Region	1860	1880	1900
United Kingdom	19.5	26.0	.7
Other Western Europe	.2	23.0	11.0
Asia[a]	7.0	4.3	20.7

Source: STRTC (1860); TBI (1880); SABI (1900). (See Table A–1 in Appendix A for list of abbreviations.)
[a] 90% to Japan.

indicative of the impoverished state of knowledge about the Victorian world economy. Wright says:

> The retardation is universally recognized by historians of the textile industry, though the reasons are not yet well understood. Britain faced increasing barriers to trade in the late nineteenth century, and such barriers may have slowed down world textiles growth, as a steadily decreasing share of textiles entered international trade. But restrictions on trade were if anything worse during 1900–1913, when the British and world textiles output again accelerated: one suspects that the causes lie deeper in the history of British economic development and its relationship to the world economy. Clearly, British home demand for cotton goods was not rising. Tyson attributes the slow growth of 1870–1900 to the decline in world prices of primary products and the resulting stagnation in purchasing power in many of Britain's major markets.[8]

Wright helps explain the decline of the British share in world consumption, but he too readily equates British demand with world demand. Indeed, demand grew faster during the late nineteenth century in the United States, continental Europe, and Asia than in Great Britain. That a retardation in growth occurred is no doubt true, but the retardation could easily have been less pronounced than Wright suggests. These points do not refute Wright, but they are of use in putting into better perspective his interpretation of the world cotton market in the late nineteenth century and his analysis of the reasons for the slowness of economic progress in the postbellum South (see Chapter 2), and they suggest that further research is needed on world demand for cotton in the nineteenth century.

This is not a complete picture of developments in the postbellum cotton market, but several themes that are subordinated in most discussions of Victorian trade in cotton are revealed to be important. One such theme is heightened competition between a developing country, the United States, and the LDCs. Another is a slowing in the growth rate of world demand for

[8]*Ibid.*, p. 633.

cotton presumably for microeconomic reasons, or at least for reasons not connected primarily with aggregate economic growth per se.[9] A third theme is the change in relative growth rates of demand for cotton in the industrializing regions. A fourth is exogenous changes on the supply side in the LDCs that were of some consequence, especially in determining relative rates of export growth among various LDCs. It will be shown that these themes are not unique to the cotton market.

Silk

A major event in the world market for raw silk during the late nineteenth century was the leftward shift in the British demand curve following the removal of import duties on manufactured silks in 1864. By 1875 imports of silk manufactures, which had been under £2 million 20 years before, exceeded £7.3 million; by 1880 they exceeded £13.3 million. After peaking at about £17 million in the 1860s, the value of domestic output of silk manufactures fell to less than £5.5 million in the early twentieth century.[10] Imports of raw silk fell from a peak of 14 million pounds in the early 1860s to 9 million pounds in the 1880s, remaining near that level for the rest of the century.

However, the price of raw silk skyrocketed during the pebrine epidemic which ravaged France's silkworm industry in the 1860s, rising over 20% between 1860 and 1870.[11] At the height of the epidemic a strong continental demand for Chinese silk appeared, offsetting to some extent the decline in British demand. But the continental market for Chinese silk dried up when the disease was overcome and domestic production of raw silk staged a comeback. In addition, Japan was emerging as a force in world markets, raising its share in world exports of raw silk from about 5% in 1860 to about 30% in 1900, and the first successful commercialization of artificial silk (rayon) took place in France in the 1890s. Presumably the rate of growth in volume of Chinese exports of raw silk during the latter decades of the century fell, or was at least lower than it would otherwise have been, although the absence of reliable statistics on the volume of Chinese exports of raw silk earlier in the century makes impossible a comparison of numerical growth rates over different periods of time.

[9]See also H. Schultz, *The Theory and Measurement of Demand* (Chicago: University of Chicago Press, 1938), chap. 8.

[10]W. Cole and P. Deane, *British Economic Growth, 1688–1959* (London: Cambridge University Press, 1968), pp. 208–209.

[11]A. Sauerbeck, "The Prices of Commodities and the Precious Metals," *Journal of the Royal Statistical Society* 48 (Sept. 1886): 646.

Nitrate of Soda

The shrinking importance of Great Britain as a buyer of LDC products is well illustrated by the case of sodium nitrate, which became the main fertilizer exported from the LDCs in part because Peruvian guano deposits were gradually used up. The volume of British imports of sodium nitrate fell by a third between the mid-1880s and the early 1900s; simultaneously, the world price of sodium nitrate fell about 25% in real terms. The combination of shrinking consumption and a falling price indicates that British demand for sodium nitrate was falling.

The decline in British demand was related to increased foreign competition. Having prospered in the middle decades of the century, British agriculture began to face stiff competition from imports. Between the early 1870s and the early 1890s annual wheat production in Great Britain fell 60% yet Great Britain remained committed to free trade. In addition, competing fertilizers were developed as a by-product of the expansion of the British gas industry. Heavier competitive pressure from non-European suppliers was also felt by continental agriculture, but most countries there raised tariffs. Germany imposed a high duty on wheat during the 1880s, and France enacted the famous Meline Tariff in 1892. The new tariffs did not stop the decline in wheat prices, but they gave agriculturalists on the Continent a certain amount of breathing room that British farmers did not have.[12]

Moreover, farmers in continental Europe were turning increasingly toward highly intensive methods of cultivation. In France alone, imports of sodium nitrate rose from 22 million francs annually in 1877–1880 to 36 million francs in 1887–1890.[13] Intensive techniques also became common elsewhere on the Continent, especially in Belgium. Furthermore, the demand for nitrates grew as a result of an expansion in European beet sugar production. Since demand for fertilizer was growing faster on the Continent than in Great Britain, a shift in the primary destinations of LDC (principally Chilean) exports of sodium nitrate resulted. But demand in North America was less expansive, in part because extensive methods of farming were practiced longer there than in Europe. In addition, the United States began to develop domestic sources of fertilizer, especially phosphates in South Carolina.

Tea and Coffee

The United Kingdom remained the world's largest market for tea throughout the Victorian era, but the rate of expansion of British tea con-

[12] I. N. Lambi, *Free Trade and Protection in Germany, 1869–1879* (Weisbaden: Franz Steinder Verlag GMBH, 1963), p. 231.
[13] E. O. Golob, *The Meline Tariff: French Agriculture and Nationalist Economic Policy* (New York: AMS Press, 1968), p. 75.

sumption fell late in the nineteenth century. Between 1840 and 1860 (or, to be precise, 1838–1842 and 1858–1862) per capita consumption in the United Kingdom doubled; between 1860 and 1880 the increase was 74%, and between 1880 and 1900, 30%. This reduction in the growth rate occurred even though the world price of tea fell over 50% between the 1870s and 1890s, a decline in real terms as well. Demand grew slowly elsewhere in the western world, where, by and large, tea was not preferred as much as it was in Great Britain.

Per capita consumption of coffee fell steadily in the United Kingdom from the 1860s on. Between 1860 and 1880 (or, to be precise, 1858–1862 and 1878–1882) annual average per capita consumption fell 25%; between 1880 and 1900 the decline was 24%. Imports of coffee did not fall until the 1870s but dropped quickly once the decline started. Consumption on the European continent and in North America was expanding rapidly, so that, of necessity, the share of LDC coffee exports absorbed by the United Kingdom shrank. Unfortunately, a more elaborate and precise quantitative description of this trend cannot be given here because of imperfections in existing data.

No attempt will be made here to explain the anomaly of declining total and per capita consumption of coffee in the British Isles while income and population were rising. But several relevant considerations can be listed.

1. The world price of coffee climbed during the last four decades of the nineteenth century. The annual average price in London was 74 shillings per hundredweight in 1858–1866 but 95 shillings in 1891–1900. The general level of prices was falling in the gold-standard world during the last quarter of the nineteenth century, implying that the rise in the real price of coffee was still greater.
2. The relative price of tea in terms of coffee fell by more than half by 1900, which probably contributed to a leftward shift in the British demand for coffee.
3. Change in preference in favor of tea that began in midcentury may have become self-sustaining as newer generations developed a taste for tea.
4. There was a slowing in the growth of British demand for other amenities, including sugar and tea, in the final decades of the century. Why this phenomenon occurred remains a mystery, but the decline in coffee consumption is probably related to it.

Sugar

The most important influences on the world sugar market in the late nineteenth century were the discovery of a way to extract more sugar from

TABLE 6.4
Distribution of Sugar Exports by Destination, Selected Countries, 1860, 1900 (millions of dollars)

	Destination							
	United Kingdom		Other Western Europe		North America		Asia	
Exporter	1860	1900	1860	1900	1860	1900	1860	1900
British Guiana	5.0	1.1	–	–	.4	4.2	–	–
British India	3.9	–	–	–	–	–	–	–
British West Indies	12.3	2.2	–	–	.2	4.1	–	–
Mauritius	7.0	.5	1.1	.1	–	.9	–	5.7
Reunion	–	–	8.0	2.0	–	–	–	–

Source: British India, SABI; British West Indies, British Guiana, and Mauritius, STRTC; Reunion, STRTFC and SY. (See Table A–1 in Appendix A for list of abbreviations.)

beets and the introduction of subsidies to beet sugar producers in the main continental European countries. In consequence, Europe, no longer producing only for local consumption, entered the world market and increased its share of world trade in sugar from zero in 1860 to approximately 60% in 1900. The world price of sugar fell over 50% during the same period. It is curious, then, that sugar consumption in the United Kingdom grew so much more slowly in the final quarter of the century than it had before that time. On a per capita basis annual average sugar consumption in the United Kingdom rose by only 34% between 1880 and 1900, whereas between 1860 and 1880 the increase had been 77%. The figures for total consumption are much the same. Obviously, British demand for sugar was expanding at a reduced rate; given certain price-elasticity conditions, it could have been falling.

With Continental producers dominating the European market and with British demand lagging, a change in the main outlets for sugar produced in the LDCs accompanied the reduction in the rate of growth in the volume of sugar marketed by them. Table 6.4 indicates the primary destinations of sugar exports from several LDCs in 1860 and 1900. A shift away from the British market and toward other regions, especially North America, is evident. The United States, however, produced a fair amount of sugar itself and was an importer of beet sugar. In addition, the price elasticity of demand for sugar in the United States during the period 1875–1895 has been estimated by Schultz to have been only −.3 to −.4.[14] The United States therefore was not from the point of view of most LDCs a completely satisfactory alternative to traditional European markets. Adamson (1972) provides direct evidence of the unsatisfactory experience one LDC, British Guiana, had with the United States market.

Rubber and Tin

In contrast to other LDC exports, rubber and tin enjoyed a booming British market near the end of the nineteenth century. Even if we allow for the increasing proportion of re-exports, British consumption of rubber rose sevenfold between 1860 and 1900, according to Table 6.5. American consumption rose equally rapidly, however, and continental Europe was not far behind. That a dramatic rightward shift in the world demand curve for rubber was taking place is further evidenced by a rise of 80% in the world price of rubber during the last quarter of the century despite deflationary conditions throughout the gold standard world.

Tin is a similar case. The real price of tin in the United Kingdom increased

[14]Schultz, *Theory and Measurement of Demand*, chap. 6.

TABLE 6.5
Total Imports and Exports of Crude Rubber from the United Kingdom,
1850–1900 (hundredweights)

Year	Imports	Exports
1850	7,617	1,048
1860	43,029	12,895
1870	152,118	50,737
1880	169,587	76,732
1890	264,008	142,524
1900	512,286	293,624

Source: Woodruff (1968, p. 46).

about 25% during the final 25 years of the nineteenth century; simultaneously, exports of tin from the Far East to Great Britain rose substantially, as Table 6.6 shows. Behind this growth in British demand lay rising world demand for tin-plate products, such as alloys for tin cans, of which Great Britain was the main supplier. In addition, by 1900 British production of tin ore was growing more slowly because of the depletion of domestic deposits.

From Table 6.6 it is seen that the growth of Straits Settlements' tin exports to the United Kingdom was greater than the growth of exports to the United States, the other major consumer, between 1880 and 1900. This may imply a centralization of this trade in the United Kingdom, in contrast to the patterns observed for many other LDC products. Although it appears that no significant swing in the tin trade away from the United Kingdom occurred, it must be remembered that Bolivia, a country for which only sketchy export data are available, was beginning to ship large quantities of tin abroad. Some of this output went to the closest large market, the United States. The main point, however, is that British demand for tin was growing at least as fast as the demand of the other industrializing regions and was presumably outstripping the growth of demand in continental Europe.

TABLE 6.6
Distribution by Destination of Tin Exports from Straits Settlements,
1880–1900 (millions of dollars)

Destination	1880	1900
United Kingdom	2.4	16.0
Other Western Europe	.2	2.5
United States	3.1	8.7
Asia	1.4	2.4

Source: STRTC. (See Table A–1 in Appendix A for list of abbreviations.)

Other Goods

JUTE

British imports of raw jute, a substitute for cotton in some products, nearly tripled during the cotton famine created by the American Civil War. Between the 1870s and 1890s, however, the volume of jute imports into Great Britain little more than doubled. With the reappearance of the United States as the chief producer of cotton, Indian jute suffered a decline in the growth rate of British demand, although the decline was less marked than that experienced by some other tropical products. In addition, jute manufacturing capacity was developed in other industrializing regions, which tended to raise non-British demand for raw jute relative to British demand.

NATURAL DYES

The LDCs' production and exports of natural dyes, including indigo and logwood, were depressed by the commercialization of synthetic dyes in Germany during the second half of the nineteenth century. The share of indigo in the world market for dyes fell from over 70% to 27% between 1860 and 1900. The value of world trade in indigo was more or less constant during the later decades of the century, although some real growth must have occurred, since prices tended to fall.[15]

COPPER

The growth of British demand for copper slowed in the later decades of the century, partly because wooden ships, which required copper sheathing for their hulls, were being replaced by iron steamers. Also, railway construction, which earlier had created a great demand for the metal, had passed its peak. Increased demand for copper in electrical products countered these negative factors to some extent, but this use of copper did not become a predominant factor in demand until the twentieth century.

Another problem for the LDCs was the entry of new suppliers into world markets. Table 6.7 indicates that by 1880 Chile no longer dominated the world market for copper. Although the United States exported only small amounts of this metal, a vigorous domestic industry developed there. In addition to using the most up-to-date methods, American copper interests also received tariff protection that, according to Taussig, they did not need.[16] Although they do not tell the complete story, slackening of British demand

---

[15]See V. Anstey, *The Economic Development of India* (London: Longmans, Green, & Co., 1939), pp. 288–289; and K. G. Ponting, "Logwood: An Interesting Dye," *Journal of European Economic History* 2 (Spring 1973): 109–119.

[16]F. W. Taussig, *The Tariff History of the United States* (New York: Augustus M. Kelley Publishers, 1967), p. 221.

TABLE 6.7
Value of Exports of Copper in Selected Countries, 1840–1900 (millions of dollars)

Country	1840	1860	1880	1900
Chile	n.a.	16.1	12.7	7.8
Cuba	5.0	–	–	–
Mexico	–	–	–	4.7
Portugal	–	–	1.9	1.2
Spain	–	1.0	11.4	9.8
United States	–	1.7	3.0	1.2

Source: Appendix D.

and the exploitation of deposits elsewhere in the world clearly are important in explaining the stagnation of Chilean copper exports after 1860.

RICE

The position of the United Kingdom as an outlet for Asian rice declined in the late nineteenth century (see Table 6.8). In the early phases of the expansion of the world rice trade, the United Kingdom was the middleman in Europe because it owned the most advanced milling equipment. But milling and port facilities were enlarged and improved in Hamburg and Bremen, with the result that leadership in the re-export trade passed from Great Britain to Germany in the last 25 years of the century.[17] The United States and Italy were also sizable rice producers, which contributed to slight growth in demand for LDC rice in other industrializing regions. Italy, in fact, annually exported rice valued at several million dollars in the late nineteenth century, making it a direct competitor of the LDCs in external markets.

COCOA

The rapid expansion of the cocoa trade at the end of the nineteenth century occurred largely in response to rising demand, since in a deflationary era the price of cocoa rose in step with expanding consumption. The annual average price per hundredweight of cocoa f.o.b. Jamaica, a good proxy for the world price, was 39.3 shillings in 1882–1884, 49.1 shillings in 1891–1893, and 52.5 shillings in 1897–1899. The destinations of of LDC cocoa exports are impossible to ascertain precisely, but it appears that North America, Other Western Europe, and Great Britain each took a healthy share. In addition to rising incomes in these countries, another

[17]A full discussion may be found in S. Cheng, *The Rice Industry of Burma, 1852–1940* (Singapore: University of Malaya Press), pp. 203–204.

TABLE 6.8
Distribution of Rice Exports by Destination for Selected Countries, 1880–1900 (millions of dollars)

					Destination					
	United Kingdom		Other Western Europe		Asia		Africa		South America	
Exporter	1880	1900	1880	1900	1880	1900	1880	1900	1880	1900
British India	18.5	5.5	–	2.8	14.2	15.5	7.6	14.8	–	1.9
Straits Settlements	–	–	–	–	5.8	10.8	–	–	–	–
Indochina	–	–	1.0	3.0	n.a.	16.0	–	–	–	–

Source: British India, TBI (1880), SABI (1900); Straits Settlements, STRTC; Indochina, TSSEA. (See Table A–1 in Appendix A for list of abbreviations.)

important reason for the expansion in world demand for cocoa must have been the falling price of sugar, a complement to cocoa in many uses, especially in the making of confectionaries.

NUTS

Most of the nut trade (primarily ground nuts) involved Other Western Europe and Tropical Africa. Rising demand must have made nuts a valuable commodity, since there were few, if any, exogenous developments on the supply side to stimulate this trade.

Supply

The possibility that changing supply conditions in the LDCs themselves contributed to the swing of their trade away from the United Kingdom and to the eventual slackening in their export growth cannot be disregarded. Still, a compelling hypothesis that would explain the changing destinations of LDC exports with reference to supply is hard to formulate. As mentioned earlier, patterns of diversification in market outlets were similar for many LDCs; it is unlikely that such consistency would have been produced by presumably unrelated changes in supply conditions all over the world.

There are, on the other hand, two plausible supply hypotheses that might help explain the decline in the growth rate of LDC exports. One, which will be called the "development hypothesis," is that economic growth in LDCs themselves drew resources from export industries into production for the domestic market. The other, which will be called the "supply constraint hypothesis," is that inelasticities in supply developed and hindered some industries in matching output with rising world demand. The latter hypothesis also encompasses the possibility that leftward shifts in supply curves occurred in the LDCs. The development and supply constraint hypotheses are not mutually incompatible; both kinds of influence might be included in a full explanation of the main trends.

The Development Hypothesis

It is doubtful that the rate of export growth fell because of rapidly growing domestic demand in the LDCs. In Chapter 2 it is pointed out that the proportion of national product represented by exports was rising in the less developed world during the second half of the nineteenth century, which is not the pattern that would be expected if rapid domestic growth were restraining exports. Leff would probably accept this reasoning for Brazil. Economic modernization may actually have stimulated the exports of some

LDCs by fostering export diversification. British India's textile industry, for example, became competitive in world markets, with the result that Indian exports of cotton manufactures and jute manufactures grew 6-fold and 20-fold in value, respectively, between 1860 and 1900. Moreover, additions to productive capacity in the LDCs often were made specifically to increase exports. For instance, improved methods of production were adopted to stimulate Egyptian cotton exports and Javan sugar exports. Although a few products might be found for which export growth was held back by domestic economic growth in certain LDCs, these would hardly be typical.

The Supply Constraint Hypothesis

COFFEE

Coffee is the only example of an important LDC product for which global supply constraints appeared during the late nineteenth century. Late in the 1860s *hemalia vestatrix,* a coffee bush disease, struck in the Far East, bringing an end to coffee production in Ceylon within three decades and a sharp drop in output in Java and British India. The post-1860 emergence of several Central American countries as major suppliers compensated only partially for losses of output in the Far East. One wonders how long it would have taken the Central American coffee industries to emerge if better-established suppliers had not run into such extreme difficulties.

In parts of Brazil "routinism" was perpetuated, and new sources of inefficiency appeared in the second half of the century. After the slave trade was terminated in 1851, the average age of the slave population of some districts increased, causing a loss in productivity. In one district only 40% of the slave labor force was of prime working age (18–40 years of age) in 1860, whereas the figure had been 60% during the 1840s.

With the abolition of slavery in 1888 came a reduction in the man-hours of labor available for the cultivation and harvesting of coffee. To some extent immigration provided an offset, but 14- and 18-hour workdays were no longer the rule for field labor, wages were higher, and productivity suffered at least temporarily as production was reorganized.[18] Another problem in Brazil was the gradual destruction of the virgin forest. In some areas soil erosion resulted from careless deforestation, and a loss of fertility occurred as well.

Despite these problems the value of Brazilian exports of coffee doubled between 1880 and 1900, which does not compare unfavorably with earlier rates of increase. But the rate of growth of volume fell. Leff's data show that the quantity of coffee exported by Brazil expanded at a rate of 3.8% per

[18]S. Stein, *Vassouras* (Cambridge, Mass.: Harvard University Press, 1957), p. 79, chap. 9.

year between 1874 and 1913, as compared with a 5.3% per year rate of increase between 1822 and 1873. The long-run supply function of Brazilian coffee evidently was less elastic late in the nineteenth century than it had been previously; consequently, Brazil could not take advantage of supply problems in the Far East, as it had in the 1840s and 1850s.

OTHER GOODS

There are several LDC products for which developments on the supply side stimulated an expansion in trade. Jamaica, previously one of the slowest regions to adopt new technology, modernized sugar production in the second half of the nineteenth century. The average annual output of Jamaican sugar factories nearly doubled between 1852 and 1869 and continued to grow thereafter.[19] The government of Java sponsored a program during the 1880s to improve irrigation facilities. Fertilizer became more widely used there, and sugar factories were fitted with new and costly machinery. Consequently, output per bouw (1.7 acres) doubled between 1870 and 1900.[20] Although the competitive position of most of the sugar-producing LDCs worsened despite efforts such as these, by the late nineteenth century at least a few LDCs were capable of great increases in productivity.

Innovation also occurred in tea production. By the late 1860s Indian plantations were using new methods in all phases of production, including plucking, withering, drying, rolling, and packing; by 1880 India had captured about 25% of the world market. Ceylon also figured significantly in the tea market late in the century, when most of its coffee plantations were converted to tea. New methods presumably were adopted there as well.

Egyptian exports also were stimulated by advances on the supply side. Official policy continued to be export oriented, and the American cotton famine raised hopes within Egypt. Hershlag writes:

> The brilliant prospects for cotton cultivation gave an impetus to westernization and development experiments. The implementation of daring town development projects was commenced; sumptuous buildings were erected; the network of canals, irrigation works, and communications and cotton gins became widespread.[21]

The reentry of the United States into world competition was, of course, unfortunate for Egypt. Yet Egyptian exports of cotton grew apace, rising

[19]G. Eisner, *Jamaica, 1830–1930: A Study in Economic Growth* (Manchester: Manchester Press, 1961), p. 302.

[20]J. S. Furnivall, *Netherlands India* (London: Cambridge University Press, 1939), p. 195.

[21]Z. Y. Hershlag, *Introduction to the Economic History of the Middle East* (Netherlands: E. J. Brill, 1964), p. 96.

600% in value between 1860 and 1880 and nearly doubling in value between 1880 and 1900.

In British India, by contrast, a collapse of excess supply occurred after 1875. A leftward shift of the supply curve of Indian cotton exports is clearly apparent in Wright's econometric results and is perhaps attributable to widespread famine and to the failure of new strains of cotton introduced during the Civil War years to acclimatize adequately. The leftward shift of the Indian supply curve of cotton exports counteracts part of the rightward shift in the Egyptian supply curve. Between 1880 and 1900, a period of declining nominal prices for cotton, the value of combined Indian and Egyptian exports of this fiber rose by about $9 million, implying a rather slow increase in the supply of tropical cotton.

Summary and Conclusions

A crucial aspect of the international economy during the late nineteenth century was the decline or slow increase in British demand for several important LDC products, including silk, cotton, sodium nitrate, coffee, sugar, and tea. Data on rates of growth of British consumption of 11 goods between 1840 and 1900 are summarized in Table 6.9. These goods amounted

TABLE 6.9

Percentage Change in British Consumption or Imports of Selected Products, 1840–1900 (volume terms)

Product	1840–1860	1860–1880	1880–1900
Coffee	18	−7	−10
Copper (imports)	n.a.	882	87
Cotton	139	32	33
Indigo (imports)	n.a.	24	−50
Jute (imports)	4500	636	132
Nitrate of soda (imports)	n.a.	750	−34
Rice (imports)	n.a.	646	−9
Silk (imports)	97	−25	0
Sugar	129	116	59
Tea	118	112	54
Wheat (imports)	263	100	41

Source: Figures for coffee, silk, sugar, tea, copper, and wheat are computed from data in Mitchell and Deane (1962); cotton computed from Sundbärg (1908); indigo, nitrate of soda, and rice computed from Sauerbeck (1886) and *Statistical Abstract of the United Kingdom* (1901); jute computed from Ahmed (1966).

Note: Figures for coffee, silk, sugar, and tea are based on 5-year averages of the data centered on years at column head; indigo, nitrate of soda, and rice are 3-year averages centered on 1849, 1873, and 1900; figures for copper (unwrought) are 5-year averages centered on 1850, 1875, and 1900; for cotton, 5-year averages centered on 1838, 1858, 1878, and 1898; for wheat, 5-year averages centered on 1842, 1862, 1882, and 1902; for jute, benchmark years are 1833, 1850, 1870, and 1890.

to about 50% of LDC exports in 1880, and Great Britain was a leading market for all of them, except possibly coffee. In every case growth was much slower later in the century, and in four instances consumption declined after 1880. Fewer LDC products experienced a surge in British demand, and they were quantitatively less significant than the others.

Several reasons for the abatement in British demand for so many key products have been listed. The immediate cause of decline in British silk manufacturing, for example, was the removal of tariff protection. The development of competitive rice-milling facilities on the continent of Europe forced the curtailment of Great Britain's re-export trade in rice. British agriculture was faced with stiff foreign competition and lacked tariff protection, with the result that British demand for fertilizer declined. Chilean copper was less in demand as wooden ships became obsolete, as growth in the railroads slowed, and as other suppliers of copper entered the British market. No firm explanation has been offered for the slackening of demand for sugar (both cane and beet), tea, and coffee, but it appears that developments within Great Britain itself were largely responsible for slower growth in demand for these goods. Another reason for slackening British demand for cane sugar was the appearance of a cheaper substitute, beet sugar.

The market potential of Other Western Europe and North America was surprisingly limited considering how expansive the economies in these regions were. Continental Europe, of course, subsidized beet sugar production, and the United States was a producer of cane sugar. Large quantities of silk, both natural and artificial, were produced in Italy and France, and Japan was becoming competitive in this fiber. Copper production became substantial in the United States and parts of Western Europe once new deposits and better methods of extraction had been discovered. American copper producers also were granted tariff protection. The United States regained competitive superiority in cotton after the Civil War and could meet most of Europe's needs. Rice was popular in the United States and Other Western Europe, but domestic production in these areas was by no means insignificant. The commercialization of synthetic dyes, especially in continental Europe, weakened world demand for natural dyes. Only a few LDC products found large, buoyant markets elsewhere once British demand began to slack off.

The list of export-stimulating or export-retarding changes on the supply side within the LDCs themselves is short. Only tea, cotton manufactures, and jute manufactures of the products discussed seem to have depended heavily on cost reductions for their expansion in trade. They were exceptional cases, albeit important ones. Similarly, few LDC products besides coffee were affected by significant supply constraints near the end of the nineteenth century. LDC entrepreneurs, by and large, seem to have had little trouble expanding or contracting output in response to price incentives.

Having reviewed the supply and demand factors affecting LDC exports, we can understand why the rate of growth of LDC exports declined in the final quarter of the nineteenth century. Large changes in costs of production within most LDC export industries were few, and, if anything, reductions predominated. Economic development within the LDCs probably did not put such heavy, across-the-board demands on LDC resources that export growth was restrained. On the demand side, the weakening demand in Great Britain, the largest single market for LDC products during the nineteenth century, for quite a few important LDC products was not fully offset by rising demand in other parts of the world. The other industrializing countries were more self-sufficient than the United Kingdom and were also in the process of encroaching on the traditional markets held by LDC producers, a point that conventional and Marxist writers seemingly fail to realize. Thus, while non-British demand for LDC goods was rising faster than British demand, it was not rising fast enough to sustain the rate of growth in aggregate LDC exports achieved earlier.

This analysis is not wholly consistent with what is sometimes called the "suction pump" theory of trade between the West and the Third World during the nineteenth century. When facets of LDC development that have previously been ignored are recognized and appreciated, it is not obvious that the industrializing countries were simply expropriators of LDC produce and raw materials. Moreover, Great Britain experienced a slowing in the growth of demand for certain LDC goods for reasons apparently unrelated to the intensification of international competition in primary products between the LDCs and some of the now-developed regions. Thus, even if the competitive factor could be ignored, the "suction pump" theory would not be precisely true, even in its own terms.

7

Tariffs, Transportation Costs, Exchange Rates, Terms of Trade, and Export Surpluses

In the preceding chapter only a few words were devoted to the impact of changes in commercial policy at the center and of falling transportation costs on LDC exports. Nor have the implications for the LDCs of possible export surpluses and changing exchange rates and terms of trade yet been discussed. The following discussion will make a few general observations on each of these formidable topics. The purpose in doing this is mainly to make a prima facie case that taking these factors into consideration does not substantially alter the analysis to this point.

Let us recall the pertinent facts. Between about 1860 and 1880 the rate of growth of LDC trade remained at roughly its earlier level of just over 4% per year, but between 1880 and 1900 the rate fell to about 3% per year. The relative decline of Great Britain as a market for LDC exports became manifest between 1860 and 1880, and between 1880 and 1900 the decline accelerated. In absolute terms, the rate of growth of LDC exports to Great Britain during the second period was probably no more than 1% per year in real terms.

Tariff Policy

The four decades between 1860 and 1900 may be divided into two periods of equal length with respect to European commercial policies, 1860–1880 and 1880–1900. During the first, a free trade policy was pursued by most of Western Europe; by the second, the Continent had returned to protectionism. This partitioning of the period 1860–1900 follows

Bairoch, who makes Germany his bellwether.[1] Other European countries, however, did not return to protectionism until later. France, for example, did not pass the Meline Tariff until 1892. Other countries in Western Europe occupy an intermediate position between Germany and France.

European tariff policies during the late nineteenth century were interdependent and were framed primarily with intra-European trade in mind. In other words, imports from the Third World were not typically subjected to marked increases in tariffs after the liberalizations of the free trade era were abandoned. Germany, for example, placed low revenue duties on tea and coffee in the 1879 tariff bill but left many raw materials, including rubber, untaxed.[2] This reflected the overall policy of making tariffs progressive by stage of manufacture. In agriculture the main duties applied to breadstuffs, of which the LDCs were minor exporters.

Tariff policy in the United States was protectionist between 1860 and 1900. Tariffs raised during the Civil War were retained and even increased by subsequent legislation. But from the LDC viewpoint American policy may have seemed less restrictive than before, or at least not any more restrictive. Duties on tea and coffee were abolished in the Tariff Act of 1872, and sugar duties were abolished in 1890 but restored a few years later. A stiff duty on copper was enacted in 1869, but it was lowered somewhat in 1883. Duties on finished goods, including some that were exported by the LDCs, were raised slightly. The general principle was to reduce or abolish purely revenue-producing duties and to retain protective duties.[3]

On the basis of this evidence, it is hard to argue that LDC exports were much affected by changes in tariffs in the leading markets, a statement that would also hold for complements of, or substitutes for, the products on which tariffs were modified. This view is reinforced by the often price-inelastic demand curves for LDC products in the industrializing regions, with little effect on quantities consumed resulting from tariff-induced price changes.

In addition to possible direct consumption effects of tariff changes, the effects of commercial policy on a country's economic development must also be considered. Perhaps the main influence of tariff policy on LDC trade was through the dynamic effects in promoting development and, in consequence, the growth of demand in some of the now-developed economies for

---

[1]P. Bairoch, "Free Trade and European Economic Development in the 19th Century," *European Economic Review* 3 (Nov. 1972); 211–245.

[2]I. N. Lambi, *Free Trade and Protection in Germany, 1869–1879* (Weisbaden: Franz Steinder Verlag GMBH, 1963), p. 175.

[3]F. W. Taussig, *The Tariff History of the United States* (New York: Augustus M. Kelley Publishers, 1967), pt. 2, chap. 3.

LDC products. But this is conjectural, since little is actually known about the dynamic gains or losses that resulted from the commercial policies of the now-developed countries, making it impossible to draw on a well-established body of knowledge for help with the problem. However, Bairoch's article, cited earlier in this section, examines some of the dynamic effects of tariff policy in Europe during the late nineteenth century and offers some clues to the general relationship between commercial policy at the center and LDC trade.

Bairoch contends that free trade led to retardation in the rate of economic growth in the continental European countries and that the return to a protectionist policy contributed to an increase in the rate of growth. For our purposes, Bairoch's most significant contention is that free trade did not hamper industrialization on the Continent but undermined the agricultural sector. Bairoch holds that with respect to trade in manufactured goods continental Europe benefited as much or more from free trade as Great Britain did but that protectionism was even better for continental Europe. "The closing of European markets at a time when free trade was still being practiced in Britain," he writes, "led to a complete reversal of trade in manufactured goods: U.K. sales marked time, whereas those of Europe continued to make speedy progress."[4] Bairoch's analysis has obvious implications for the behavior of world demand for jute, cotton, silk, and other basic inputs into manufactures.

The evidence suggests that tariff policy in the United States and continental Europe vis-à-vis the LDCs may have been slightly liberalized after about 1860 and that tariff policy vis-à-vis Great Britain was loosened only temporarily, to Britain's ultimate detriment. This pattern of tariff changes contributed directly and indirectly to the decline in Great Britain's relative position as a buyer of LDC products and to the rise in the positions of North America and Other Western Europe. Tariff policy probably had little effect on the growth rate of LDC exports, however, since duties on products from Asia, Africa, and Latin America were raised or lowered by small amounts in most cases. Furthermore, the positive effect on LDC exports of tariff-stimulated economic growth in protectionist countries was offset to some extent by slackening of demand in Great Britain, the country most disadvantaged by protectionism.

Pending further research, the most reasonable conclusion is that in and of themselves tariffs may have operated either to raise or to lower the growth rate of LDC exports but that the net effect in either case probably was small.

---

[4]Bairoch, "Free Trade and Economic Development," p. 239.

International Transportation Costs

It is well known that international transportation costs plummeted during the second half of the nineteenth century. The question is whether the cheapening of freight rates was of primary or secondary importance in determining the main trends in LDC exports. There is scope for much useful research in this area, but, in my view, falling transportation costs are of little help in answering the main questions with which this book is concerned.

One reason for discounting the importance of falling transportation costs is that there is no evidence of any speed-up in the growth of LDC trade during the period when transportation costs were undergoing their most pronounced decline. In fact, the rate of growth of LDC exports fell. On the micro level, Ingram makes similar observations about rice exports from Thailand.[5] He finds no evidence that the opening of the Suez Canal in 1869 led to more rapid expansion of Thailand's rice exports to Europe. An obvious reason why the stimulatory effect of falling transportation costs on the volume of LDC exports would have been muted is the price-inelasticity of demand for some LDC products in the industrializing regions.

Late-century trends in intra-Asian trade are another reason why falling transportation costs presumably are of secondary importance. If falling long-distance freight rates were indeed a major contributor to greater interdependence in the world economy, it might have been expected that intra-Asian exports would fall as a proportion of all Asian trade. In fact, the proportion rose from 30% in 1860 to 37% in 1900. If Japan is excluded as a recipient of exports from the Asian LDCs, the proportion falls modestly from 30% to 28%. Few historians would argue that falling freight rates operated differentially to increase intra-Asian trade at the expense of trade with the center. It would appear, then, that Asian demand for Asian products was rising about as fast as demand at the center. Since this conclusion holds even when Japan, by far the most dynamic country in the region, is ignored, one must infer that demand at the center was weak.

A final reason for questioning the importance of declining freight rates is that one of the most important claims made on behalf of the transportation revolution—diversification of LDC exports—has been much exaggerated in past studies. The commodity composition of LDC exports changed little after 1860 for reasons suggested earlier. Moreover, much of the diversification that did take place can hardly be ascribed to better transportation. Can the spectacular growth of British India's exports of cotton and jute manufactures, for example, really be attributed to lower freight rates?

[5] J. Ingram, *Economic Change in Thailand Since 1850* (Stanford, Calif.: Stanford University Press, 1955), p. 42.

Exchange Rates

The relevant question to ask concerning the behavior of exchange rates in the LDCs and of official exchange-rate policy in these countries after about 1860 is whether the net effect was to stimulate or to retard the growth of aggregate exports. Although individual countries might have been able to manipulate their exchange rates to achieve a competitive advantage for their exports, the benefits thus achieved could have been easily offset by the losses to other LDCs. Since most countries were on the gold standard, however, there presumably was little scope for the manipulation of exchange-rate policy, as the case of deficit-plagued Colombia attests.[6]

Nugent has shown, on the other hand, that countries on the silver standard experienced a long-run depreciation of their currencies because of the secular decline in the gold price of silver during the late nineteenth century.[7] He argues that in consequence their export performance improved in comparison with that of countries on gold. His main evidence consists of several remarkable tables showing that the annual average rate of growth of exports from countries on the silver standard during the period 1875–1895 was four times as great as the annual growth rate for countries on the gold standard (4% per year versus 1% per year). Of the 18 countries in Nugent's main table of silver-standard countries, 17 are in the LDC category and represent roughly 50% of LDC trade. If the accelerated export growth of the silver-standard LDCs did not come at the expense of reduced export growth for LDCs on gold, Nugent's argument implies that the exports of the LDCs taken together would have received a boost from the decline in the price of silver in terms of gold.

I have argued in an earlier article that notwithstanding Nugent's striking empirical finding, it is unlikely that the depreciation of the currencies of the silver standard countries accounts for much, if any, of the difference in export performance between these countries and those on the gold standard.[8] What is of greater interest for the present discussion, however, is that movements in exchange rates probably did not contribute to *retardation* in the export growth of the silver-standard countries. The depreciation of currencies tied to silver could have been a positive force in the export expansion of some countries and perhaps a positive force in the expansion of LDC exports taken as a whole, although this latter proposition is ques-

[6]See W. P. McGreevey, *An Economic History of Colombia, 1845–1930* (London: Cambridge University Press, 1971).

[7]J. B. Nugent, "Exchange-Rate Movements and Economic Development in the Late Nineteenth Century," *Journal of Political Economy* 81 (Sept./Oct. 1973): 1110–1135.

[8]J. R. Hanson II, "Exchange-Rate Movements and Economic Development in the Late Nineteenth Century: A Critique," *ibid.* 83 (July/Aug. 1975): 859–862.

tionable. At the least, the effect of exchange-rate movements on the growth rate of aggregate LDC exports would have been neutral.

Terms of Trade

The terms of trade are interesting for other reasons than the rest of the variables discussed in this chapter. The other variables are determinants of real export performance, whereas the terms of trade reflect the purchasing power of a given quantity of exports in terms of imports. Since a major theme of this book is that a retardation of demand at the center occurred in the late nineteenth century, it is nevertheless appropriate to ask whether any offset to slower export growth was provided by improvements in the terms of trade.

Evidence on the behavior of the terms of trade of the LDCs during the nineteenth century is sketchy indeed. It is this lack of information that led to the now-discredited practice of viewing the British terms of trade as the reciprocal of the terms of trade of the tropical world. Taking a different but also sweeping tack, Bairoch argues that the terms of trade of the Third World improved steadily between the 1870s and the 1930s.[9] Using an index of the price of manufactures developed by Lewis, Stover further reports that for 11 key tropical commodities the commodity terms of trade in the late nineteenth century fell in four cases, rose in six cases, and were constant in one case.[10] These results are not inconsistent with Bairoch, although they leave the impression that the picture was mixed.

The few estimates of the terms of trade available for specific LDCs also show a variety of experience in the late nineteenth century. Leff, for example, couches his discussion of Brazilian export performance in the income terms of trade and not in the value of exports. His conclusion that exports grew slowly is reached in full cognizance that, on his best estimate, Brazil experienced a steady improvement in its terms of trade. British India experienced a long-term improvement in both its net barter and income terms of trade during the second half of the nineteenth century.[11] Jamaica's gross barter terms of trade fluctuated between 1850 and 1910, according to Eisner's estimates, but deteriorated on balance.[12] This is the pattern one

[9]P. Bairoch, *The Economic Development of the Third World Since 1900* (London: Methuen & Co., 1975), pp. 859–862.

[10]C. Stover, "Tropical Exports," in *Tropical Development, 1880–1913,* ed. W. A. Lewis (Evanston: Northwestern University Press, 1970), p. 51.

[11]B. M. Bhatia, "Terms of Trade and Economic Development: A Case Study of India—1861–1939," *Indian Economic Journal* 16 (Apr./June 1969): 414–433.

[12]G. Eisner, *Jamaica, 1830–1930: A Study in Economic Growth* (Manchester: Manchester University Press, 1961), chap. 13.

should also expect to find in economies based on cane sugar, such as British Guiana and Mauritius.

Although our knowledge of the historical behavior of the terms of trade of the LDCs is fragmentary, one preliminary conclusion may be drawn from this evidence. If the real growth of LDC exports was depressed by slowing growth in world demand in the latter part of the nineteenth century, it is unlikely that unfavorable movements in the terms of trade would have done much to accentuate the harm to most economies. Growth in Brazil's import capacity was slow, even though its terms of trade were improving, a statement that would surely hold for British India as well. Jamaica's main problem was not its terms of trade. For the beleaguered sugar economies, deterioration in the terms of trade would have been but an insult added to a critical injury. Of course, Bairoch's opinion cannot be ignored. The most balanced view, then, is that changes in the terms of trade probably did not accentuate the basic problems the LDCs had in the international sphere.

Export Surpluses

It frequently is argued that for a variety of reasons the LDCs traditionally received less than their fair share of the gains arising from trade between them and the now-developed countries of Europe and North America. One reason sometimes given is that historically a large portion of export earnings was set aside for income remittances by immigrant labor, for repatriation of business profits and foreign capital, and for payment of interest and dividends on foreign investment, with the result that much of the import potential of LDCs was drained off. Indeed, an actual physical loss supposedly was suffered, since an export surplus was necessary to provide the funds for remittance abroad. This proposition, which is not of recent vintage, has seen a renewal of interest lately with the publication of an article by Andre Gunder Frank making the exploitation case and a telling rejoinder by A. J. H. Latham pointing out that neither nineteenth-century India nor China, countries Frank uses to illustrate his case, are good examples of the type of exploitation Frank describes.[13]

We can broaden the frame of reference in this debate by presenting new data concerning import and export surpluses during the nineteenth century for a disaggregated sample of countries. Frank's approach, in general, is a highly aggregative one, but the *Statistical Abstract of Foreign Countries*

---

[13]Andre Gunder Frank, "Multilateral Merchandise Trade Imbalances and Uneven Economic Development," *Journal of European Economic History* 5 (1976): 407–438; A. J. H. Latham, "Merchandise Trade Imbalances and Uneven Economic Development in India and China," *ibid.* 7 (1978): 33–60.

contains time series of imports and exports extending well back into the nineteenth century for some 60 countries.[14] For some of these countries flows of precious metals are also recorded for at least part of the period covered by the trade data. Using the data in the *Abstract* it is possible to develop a picture of the state of the trade balance for many LDCs during the late nineteenth and early twentieth centuries. For some countries the impact of the trade balance on financial flows can also be gauged using the data on the movement of precious metals.

In what follows, Latham's criteria for evaluating Frank's argument will be applied, and one criterion will be added. The main question to be asked is the following: Did most LDCs experience a perennial export surplus on merchandise account through the early twentieth century? In those countries that did, is it also true that remittances abroad typically used up the surplus, so that a net loss of the precious metals occurred? An export surplus is not necessarily bad, of course. Some countries in the modern world, such as the United States, worry about persistent import surpluses, an attitude Frank might find hard to understand. The question here, though, is merely the factual one of whether the typical LDC had a persistent export surplus during what is generally considered to be a Europe-dominated phase in the evolution of the modern international economic order. In addition, it is useful to speculate about what percentage of the national product of the LDCs might have been "lost" through chronic, uncompensated export surpluses, a topic neither Frank nor Latham discusses.

Sources and Data

For our purposes, the main problem with the *Abstract* is that in addition to containing data covering different lengths of time depending on the country, some of the merchandise export and import data include exports and imports of precious metals for all or part of the period covered by the time series. Since the *Abstract* usually specifies the years when this situation exists, the practice was followed of using merchandise data dating from the year flows of precious metals were separated statistically from the other flows. When no guidelines were explicit in the *Abstract,* it was assumed that the trade data referred to merchandise alone. Actually, these procedures do not greatly change the impressions derived from the edited data, as compared with ones based on an uncritical acceptance of the raw data.

A country occasionally had to be omitted because the official data were either obviously unreliable or unusable for some other reason, such as large

[14]United States Department of Commerce and Labor, *Statistical Abstract of Foreign Coun tries,* Washington, D.C.: U.S. Government Printing Office, 1909.

gaps in the series. Colombia is one such country. McGreevey, however, has supplied estimates of Colombia's trade balance during the nineteenth century.[15] If these were included here, the argument presented below would be strengthened. The Straits Settlements also were excluded, because of their entrepôt status. Taken at face value, however, the data for the Straits Settlement included in the *Abstract* also support the conclusions drawn here. The minor adjustments made in the data do not in any way bias the argument against Frank's thesis.

Results

The main issues in the Frank–Latham dispute are whether the typical LDC experienced a chronic export surplus during the late nineteenth and early twentieth centuries and, if so, whether this surplus was used up in the financing of remittances abroad, especially the returns on foreign investment in the LDCs. Another possible question is whether the export surplus (assuming there was one) represented a large share of exports and/or national product in the typical LDC. In other words, the physical loss that Frank claims the LDCs suffered on account of chronic export surpluses might have been small, in which case Frank's argument would be irrelevant for all practical purposes.

The relevant historical data for 34 LDCs are set forth in Table 7.1. The column headings are self-explanatory. It will be noted that for most of the countries the length of the time series of trade data is rather long; for some, the number of years covered exceeds 50. Moreover, the raw data provided by the *Abstract* are in a few cases more comprehensive than the data summarized in the table. But, to repeat, no attempt has been made to slant the data in one direction or another. Since the data summarized in the table are as usable as it is possible for a contemporary scholar to make them, there are additional grounds for confidence in the inferences to be drawn from them.

According to the table, 19 of the 34 countries experienced an export surplus during less than half of the years covered by the data. All but one of these 19 countries experienced a cumulative import surplus during the period covered in the table. The countries having an import surplus were as disparate and widely separated from each other as, for example, Martinique, China, and Tunis. If we follow Frank in regarding export surpluses as a burden to a developing country, then, historically, a great many of today's LDCs did not have this problem.

Sixteen countries listed in the table had a cumulative export surplus; they are the potential victims of the exploitation Frank describes. For eight of

TABLE 7.1
Historical Balance of Payments Data, Various Countries

Country	(1) Period	(2) Number of years	(3) Number of years with export surplus	(4) Cumulative export surplus (+) or import surplus (−) on merchandise account (millions of dollars)	(5) Cumulative export surplus as proportion of cumulative exports	(6) Cumulative inflow (−) or outflow (+) of precious metals (millions of dollars)
Central America						
Bahamas	1850–1906	57	1	−10.0		
Barbados	1892–1906	15	0	−17.1		
Bermuda	1893–1906	14	0	−23.9		
British Honduras	1850–1906	58	38	+11.9	.16	+2.0
Costa Rica	1883–1907	25	15	+5.5	.04	
Dutch Guiana	1850–1906	29	4	−10.4		
Grenada	1850–1906	57	42	+8.6	.17	
Guadeloupe	1880–1906	27	13	+2.9	.03	
Jamaica	1877–1906	30	7	−20.7		
Leeward Islands	1892–1906	15	6	−.5		
Martinique	1850–1906	57	11	−35.7		
Mexico	1885–1907	20	0	−472.3	.20	
Nicaragua	1897–1906	10	10	+6.5		
St. Lucia	1887–1906	20	2	−11.5		
St. Vincent	1850–1906	57	43	+4.7	.12	
Trinidad	1866–1906	41	25	+6.4	.02	−3.7

124

South America						
Brazil	1901–1906	6	6	+446.7	.37	
British Guiana	1850–1906	54	47	+98.0	.19	−1.5
Chile	1844–1906	63	45	+374.6	.15	
French Guiana	1882–1906	25	5	−12.9		
Asia						
British India	1850–1908	59	59	+5851.3	.35	−2827.5
Ceylon	1850–1907	57	17	−61.0		
China	1864–1907	44	7	−1338.5		
Dutch East Indies	1876–1906	31	31	+731.9	.27	−130.1
French Indochina	1881–1906	26	13	−34.1		
Korea	1894–1907	14	0	−67.8		
Philippines	1883–1907	25	19	+45.2	.09	+24.2
Siam	1895–1906	12	12	+58.7	.25	−30.9
Africa						
Algeria	1880–1907	28	3	−266.7		
Egypt	1879–1906	27	26	+261.9	.13	−249.5
Madagascar	1883–1906	24	6	−40.2		
Mauritius	1890–1906	17	8	+1.9	.01	
Natal	1890–1907	18	0	−454.0		
Tunis	1892–1906	15	0	−37.8		

Source: See text of chapter, p. 121.

Note: Occasionally, as in the case of British Guiana, a gap exists in the export and/or import time series, so that the number of years covered is not identical with the number of years between and including the starting and ending points of the series as given in Column 2. The data on bullion and specie flows for British Honduras and British Guiana pertain to 1882–1907 and 1879–1885, respectively. The figures for the Dutch East Indies represent specie flows only. Bullion is not included in the official statistics for that country. Countries such as Mexico and British Guiana were exporters of domestically produced precious metals during at least part of the periods covered in the table. The figures in Columns 3 and 4 are derived from data excluding the export of precious metals.

these countries the *Abstract* contains time series on flows of precious metals analogous to the series used by Latham in his discussion of British India. As Latham points out, a net inflow of precious metals in a country having an export surplus (e.g., British India) implies that the surplus was not fully committed to the making of foreign remittances. Examining the eight entries in Column 6 we see that six countries experienced a secular net inflow of precious metals. Removing the three countries for which the data on specie and bullion flows are incomplete or otherwise imperfect (i.e., British Honduras, British Guiana, Dutch East Indies) leaves five countries, of which four experienced a cumulative net inflow of precious metals. Although it would be preferable to have more complete data, these figures at least demonstrate that British India was not alone in being able to retain part of its export surplus.

In sum, 18 of the 34 countries in Table 7.1 had a cumulative import surplus, and perhaps as many as 6 others (and no fewer than 4) managed to retain a substantial part of their cumulative export surplus. There probably were others that would fit into one or the other of these categories.[16] Thus, a maximum of 12 countries, or only one-third of the countries in the table, fits Frank's description of being in a perpetual state of export surplus and possibly suffering a physical loss as a result. The question now becomes: How large was the actual loss in these remaining cases?

Column 5 shows cumulative export surpluses as a proportion of cumulative exports for the 16 countries that had such a surplus. It will be noted immediately that the proportion ranges from a low of .01 in the case of Mauritius to a high of .37 in the case of Brazil. The question is where to draw the line between a low and probably insignificant figure and a high and potentially dangerous figure. Frank does not discuss this question, but variants of it are often treated in the historical literature on the LDCs. Myint, a respected authority, says:

> In the backward countries . . . due to foreign investment and immigrant labor, a substantial part of these [export] earnings has had to be remitted abroad in the form of export surpluses on the trade account. Since these export surpluses are frequently as large as a quarter to a half of the total value of exports and since they continue [at this level] for decades, the question of sharing the earnings from the total volume of exports looms [large].[17]

Myint's generalization to the contrary notwithstanding, the table indicates that only 4 countries (Brazil, British India, Dutch East Indies, and

[16]Colombia, for example.

[17]Hla Myint, "The Gains from International Trade and the Backward Countries," in H. Myint, *Economic Theory and the Underdeveloped Countries* (New York: Oxford University Press, 1971), p. 96.

Siam) fit the pattern of experiencing export surpluses amounting to 25% or more of total exports during the period covered by the data. Four countries (Trinidad, Costa Rica, Guadeloupe, Mauritius) had extremely low surpluses as a proportion of exports, whereas the rest fall somewhere between the two extremes. If we remove these 4, the number of countries with a possibly serious exploitation problem becomes 12. The number falls to 8 (British Honduras, Grenada, St. Vincent, Brazil, Chile, British Guiana, Philippines, Nicaragua) if British India, the Dutch East Indies, Siam, and Egypt are removed by virtue of having had a net inflow of precious metals. As noted earlier in this chapter, the imperfections in the data make it impossible to render a precise accounting. Perhaps it is safest to repeat that of the countries listed in Table 7.1 no more than (and probably less than) a third provide even rough illustrations of Frank's argument.

A more sophisticated approach to estimating the potential burden of a perennial export surplus would be to measure the surplus as a percentage of national output or product. For example, if exports represented 10% of national product in a given country and the export surplus represented 10% of exports, then the export surplus would represent about 1% (i.e., 10% × 10%) of national product. In the cases of Trinidad, Costa Rica, Guadeloupe, and Mauritius, the share of product represented by the surplus probably was small, since the export surplus was such a small fraction of total exports. The situation is harder to assess in other cases. We know little, after all, about how large a proportion of total economic activity was represented by the export sector in the LDCs during the nineteenth century and how this proportion changed over time. It is argued earlier, however, that if per capita exports are any guide, then at least a few poor countries, including Honduras, Nicaragua, and British India, probably did not have large export sectors during much of the nineteenth century. According to Maddison, British India's exports amounted to about 11% of national output in 1913, the all-time high.[18] Applying this figure to earlier years implies that British India's export surplus amounted to less than 4% (35% × 11%) of national product during the second half of the nineteenth century, which was perhaps not a crushing burden, even if British India's ability to retain much of the revenue generated by its export surplus for domestic purposes is ignored. Although we can only speculate about the situation in other LDCs, a distinct possibility does exist that even in countries that experienced a perennial export surplus and that were unable to retain part of the surplus, the resulting loss of national product to foreigners was not so large as to provide a very powerful explanation of why these countries failed to achieve economic development.

[18]Angus Maddison, *Class Structure and Economic Growth* (New York: W. W. Norton & Co., 1971), p. 59.

Perhaps Frank's valid point that many of today's now-developed countries had regular import surpluses during the nineteenth century should be reiterated. Some of these nations, however, had export surpluses over certain periods of time. Examples are Austria–Hungary during most of the nineteenth century and the United States from roughly the 1870s through the early 1900s, a period during which the United States was also a net exporter of precious metals. Argentina, a nineteenth-century success story, had frequent export surpluses during the Victorian era, especially after 1890. New Zealand also experienced perennial export surpluses dating from the same period and was a net exporter of precious metals. In sum, although it is true to say that now-developed countries often had import surpluses on mechandise account during the early phases of their economic development, correlations between the existence of an import surplus and economic development and between the existence of an export surplus and lack of development are by no means perfect. Pat generalizations on this subject are likely to be wrong. Students of the historical relationship between trade and economic development are best advised to pursue their investigations on a case-by-case basis.

8
Summary and Conclusions

One of the main themes of this book has been that the preoccupation of scholars with domestic conditions that frustrate export-led development cannot be divorced from the expansive conception of the pre-World War I international economy pervading the work of both orthodox and Marxist writers. The conventional view is flawed, however, and what is thought to be a more realistic view has been presented in this book. But further research will be required to flesh out the descriptions offered and to confirm or disconfirm the economic interpretations advanced in earlier chapters.

Historical Interpretation

The most widely accepted accounts of the Victorian expansion of the international economy focus on the second half of the nineteenth century and imply that most LDCs were outside the network of trade until then. Actually, the exports of the LDCs expanded in parallel with the rest of world trade, and most LDCs had entered the network of trade by the time most accounts begin the story. The post-1860 era was different, nevertheless, in three important respects from immediately preceding decades: (1) the rate of growth of LDC exports declined after rising earlier; (2) Great Britain's share in the exports of the LDCs began to fall; and most significantly (3) the LDCs faced increasing competition in many of their specialties from the now-developed countries.

The interpretative part of this study tries to explain, among other things, why the acceleration of growth in LDC trade, especially after 1840, was associated with a tendency toward the centralization of trade in Great Britain and why the decentralization of LDC trade after about 1860 should have been associated with a reduction in the rate of export growth. Although the initial expansion in LDC exports appears to have been due mainly to rising demand stemming from the rapid growth of income and population in all the developing regions, the further increase in the rate of growth around 1840 was in large part the result of economic changes mainly affecting Great Britain. This nation began to exhaust its domestic supplies of several resouces, including copper and fertile land, in the 1830s, with the result that demand for these resources or, in the case of land, for fertilizer was felt by a wider range of LDCs than previously. At the same time, Great Britain was becoming dissatisfied with its commercial policy toward those LDCs that were its traditional trading partners. Deterioration of supply conditions in the British West Indies had left that region unable to meet rising demand for sugar and coffee, and high tariffs on non-Empire sugar and coffee had delayed the expansion of exports of these goods from other LDCs. Thus, the shift toward a free trade policy contributed to a transfer of British demand from the West Indies to other countries, to more rapid growth in aggregate LDC exports, and to a more tightly knit international economy.

By about 1860 the stage appeared to be set for even speedier growth in LDC exports. The British had removed many commercial restraints to trade, and continental Europe was preparing to follow suit. Steam-powered shipping was becoming economical, the Suez Canal would be opened within a decade, and rates of growth in population and income were high in other parts of the world besides Great Britain. But, surprisingly, an increase in the rate of growth of LDC trade did not happen. Instead, there was temporary steadiness and then decline after 1875 or 1880.

Signs of slackening British demand for LDC products began to appear after 1860. Coffee consumption declined on both a total and per capita basis, the silk industry began to slip, and growth in the consumption of tea and sugar was less vigorous. These developments and others contributed to greater diversification of market outlets for the LDCs, but the rate of growth of LDC exports remained near its previous level for a time, in large part because the growth of British demand for other products was still fairly rapid.

After about 1880 demand in Great Britain for LDC products slackened further. Demand for coffee continued to fall, and demand for sugar and tea rose only slowly. Demand for Chilean copper became less expansive with the obsolescence of wooden ships and with the entrance of other countries on the supply side of the world market. British farmers were hurt by agricultural imports, which contributed to the decline in their demand for foreign fertilizer. The silk industry continued to face stiff French competition, which undermined its demand for raw silk. Great Britain also faced heightened competition in cotton textiles and rice milling, which helped reduce the growth rate of British demand for cotton and rice.

Demand for LDC products in Other Western Europe and North America did not increase fast enough to fully offset the losses the LDCs suffered in the British market. One important reason was the self-sufficiency of the other developing regions. The United States was the world's foremost producer of cotton, Italy and France produced large amounts of silk, beet sugar from the continent of Europe largely supplanted cane sugar in world markets, and rice was grown in both Europe and the United States. Other LDC exports that were also produced in now-developed countries included wheat, textiles, tobacco, linseed, hides, and skins. It is possible as well that the rate of growth of total demand for LDC products in North America and Other Western Europe was also lower after 1880, but the evidence is lacking at present to support such a strong assertion.

Other forces moderating the growth of exports existed within the LDCs themselves. Several unfortunate events, such as the Asian coffee blight, hindered exports from some countries. In parts of Brazil efficiency in coffee production diminished. The growth and development of cotton and jute manufacturing industries in British India may have slowed the rate of growth of Indian exports of raw cotton and raw jute. But there were offsetting cost reductions in some products. British India added cotton and jute manufactures to its exports, advances were made in tea production in both Ceylon and British India, and improved methods of producing sugar were adopted in several LDCs, including Java, Jamaica, and British Guiana. The positive and negative influences of changes in supply conditions may well have offset each other as far as the aggregate exports of the LDCs are concerned.

Analytically, the main implication of this interpretation is that the rate of growth of the external stimulus to economic development in Asia, Africa, and Latin America diminished as the nineteenth century progressed. The growth of foreign demand was rapid in the middle decades of the century, but during this period export sectors in most of the LDCs must have been small, muting the impact of this demand on overall economic development. As the orientation of the LDCs to trade increased, the growth rate of foreign demand happened to fall. It is a strange coincidence that some LDCs that had large export sectors and therefore had a good chance to benefit from growth in demand for primary products experienced the greatest slackening in the growth of demand. The sugar economies best illustrate this point, but countries such as Chile, Ceylon, and Egypt also fit the pattern.

Under the circumstances, it is doubtful that large dynamic gains from trade could have accrued to most of the LDCs during the nineteenth century even if the domestic linkages between the external stimulus and internal development had functioned efficiently. Furthermore, the analysis given above renders the accusation that potential gains from trade were stolen from the LDCs by the advanced nations and that in consequence great harm was done to the LDCs somewhat less plausible, since trade has been portrayed here as just one potential contributor to economic development and perhaps not even a major one. Perhaps Leff's assessment of the Brazilian case has wider applicability. He writes:

> On the one hand, we have seen that nineteenth-century trade had only limited effects in promoting generalized development in the Brazilian economy. At the same time, expanding exports, coming concurrently with improved terms of trade, were perhaps the major source of income growth in an otherwise relatively stagnant economy.[1]

In sum, the expansion of the world economy dating from the early decades of the nineteenth century may have been historic and spectacular, but it was probably insufficient to improve the prospects for most of the millions of people living in Asia, Africa, and Latin America to enjoy the fruits of export-led economic development, even in the absence of exploitative behavior by advanced nations. Furthermore, international contacts played such a small role in the economic life of many LDCs that exploitation by foreigners through trade can hardly be a complete explanation of how the LDCs came to be impoverished by modern standards.

This argument, incidentally, is compatible with recent analyses that challenge the importance of foreign trade in the economic development of several regions of recent settlement before World War I. Especially noteworthy are the study of Canada by Chambers and Gordon and the study of the United States by Kravis.[2] Historically, trade has been more often a handmaiden of growth (to use Kravis's phrase) and not the engine of growth for most of the non-European world.

Further Research

There are two main ways of pursuing the question of why international trade failed to generate export-led development in the LDCs during the

[1] N. Leff, "Tropical Trade and Development in the Nineteenth Century: The Brazilian Experience," *Journal of Political Economy* 81 (May/June 1973): 691.

[2] E. J. Chambers and D. F. Gordon, "Primary Products and Economic Growth: An Empirical Measurement," *ibid.* 74 (Aug. 1966): 315–332; I. B. Kravis, "The Role of Exports in Nineteenth-Century United States Growth," *Economic Development and Cultural Change* 20 (Apr. 1972): 387–405.

nineteenth century. One is through additional studies of individual countries; the other is through studies of world market conditions for the products the LDCs specialized in. Both kinds of research are necessary, but in my opinion there is a greater scarcity of market studies.

One inherent problem in the individual-country-study approach is that, depending on one's politics and values, there is always the temptation to begin by asking, "What is wrong with this country?" or "How was this country exploited?" It is easy, for instance, to jump to the conclusion that the lack of internal responsiveness to the export stimulus explains slow or negligible increases in standards of living. Even the best treatments adopting the single-nation perspective, such as Leff's study of Brazil, beg important questions. If Brazil's problem was slow export growth, why did exports grow slowly? Leff's implicit answer of weak foreign demand raises questions about the international market and pushes the discussion to another level.

Perhaps the most useful function of the individual-country study is to trace the LDC experience in quantitative terms. Scholars have not fully exploited the data that were collected about many aspects of economic life in the LDCs during the nineteenth century. They could do more in tracing the behavior of such indices of modernization as per capita income, literacy ratios, mortality conditions, government expenditures on infrastructure formation, and so forth. It would be wise to clarify the facts prior to entertaining large hypotheses about the reasons for any particular country's underdevelopment.

A fine work on world market conditions for a tropical product in the nineteenth century is Wright's on cotton. There is great potential in his approach for answering about the underdeveloped world questions similar to those he asked about the South. Rigorous studies, econometric or otherwise, of world markets for copper, nitrate of soda, tea, coffee, and other LDC products should be forthcoming, if not from Wright then from someone else. Not the least of the uses of such work would be in testing the market models proposed here.

This study also has raised new issues for investigation. For example, we need to know much more about the period 1900–1913. World and LDC trade grew at high rates during these years, and even though cyclical factors were involved in this upswing, there probably were fundamental forces at work as well. Many goods came into the export structures of the now-developed countries that were not present in 1880. Motorcycles, bicycles, sewing machines, and various kinds of engines are but a few examples. In the LDCs the changes were not as drastic, but exports of rubber and tin surged in this period, petroleum began to be exported from Indonesia, and copper experienced a resurgence in trade as electricity was commercialized.

The Second Industrial Revolution influenced the trade of both the industrializing countries and the LDCs in new and as yet unexplained ways.

The subject of competition among the LDCs has not been explored in any detail as yet. Clearly, entrepreneurs in the LDCs were aware of cost conditions in other LDCs, but little is known about how they responded to supply changes in other countries and how the exports and national income of individual LDCs were affected as a result. Morgan has suggested that intra-LDC competition in the twentieth century in commercial crops has tended to push some LDCs back toward subsistence agriculture.[3]

Finally, a study of the imports of the LDCs in the nineteenth century is needed. The first task would be the collection of the relevant data, potentially a major contribution in itself. After that an analysis could be undertaken with special reference to the relation between the product composition of imports and changes in economic structure in the LDCs.

[3]T. Morgan, *Economic Development* (New York: Harper & Row, 1975), p. 301.

Reference Tables for Chapter 2

Table A-1

List of Abbreviations of Titles of Sources

STRTC   -   Statistical Tables Relating to the Colonial and Other Possessions
             of the United Kingdom (title varies)

STRTFC   -   (Statistical) Tables Relating to Foreign Countries (U.K.)

UKSAC   -   Statistical Abstract of Colonies (title varies)

UKSAFC   -   Statistical Abstract of Foreign Countries (U.K.)

USSAFC   -   Statistical Abstract of Foreign Countries (U.S.)

CRFC   -   Commercial Relations of the United States with Foreign Countries

EXDF   -   Exports, Domestic and Foreign, of the United States, 1789-1883

SABI   -   Statistical Abstract of British India

M-CS   -   Commercial Statistics

SY   -   Statesman's Yearbook

MUL   -   Dictionary of Statistics (1888)

WEBB   -   Dictionary of Statistics (1911)

TUKFC   -   Trade of the United Kingdom with Foreign Countries

TBI   -   Trade of British India with Foreign Countries and British Posessions

TSSEA   -   Trade and Shipping of Southeast Asia

ABHS   -   Abstract of British Historical Statistics

SUND   -   Apercus Statistique Internationaux (Sundbärg)

Note: In the tables that follow the source and the appropriate year are given
to identify the location of the data presented. Some of the sources,
unfortunately, cannot be found in every library. The libraries I relied
on were the Van Pelt Library of the University of Pennsylvania and the
Library of Congress. As a matter of fact, STRTFC was found as a supplement to the Parliamentary Papers in Van Pelt Library even though it was
not listed in the master index to PP nor in the general card catalogue.

Table A-2

Nineteenth-Century Exchange Rates in Terms of U.S. Dollar

	1860	1880	1900
Austrian florin	$ .50		
Belgian franc	.20		
French franc	.20		
German mark		.25	
Dutch guilder	.40		
Greek drachma	.17		
Portuguese milreis	1.08		
Spanish peseta	.20		
Russian rouble	.68	.50	
Swiss franc	.20		
Swedish krone	.26		
Danish krone	.26		
Norwegian krone	.26		
Italian lira	.20		
Turkish piastre	.05		
Romanian lei	.20		
British pound	4.86		
Brazilian milreis	.54		.19
Argentinian peso		1.00	
Peruvian dollar	1.00		
Uruguayan dollar	.84	1.00	
Chilean peso	1.00		
Mexican peso	1.00		
Japanese yen		1.00	.50
Chinese tael	1.60	1.40	
Chinese dollar	1.10		
Indian rupee			.33
Ceylon rupee			.33
Egyptian piastre	.05		
Mauritius rupee			.33

Notes: The main rates used in conversions were the 1860 rates
(which were used for 1840, also). For later years it was less
necessary to make my own conversions, since the sources frequently
had done it for me, but some later rates are presented for the
sake of interest.

Table A-3

Value of Exports Selected Countries 1840 - 1900

(millions of dollars)

	1840	1860	1880	1900
United Kingdom	250.2	661.3	1,085.5	1,417.1
Other Western Europe				
Austria-Hungary	54.0	128.8	275.1	394.4
Belgium	26.9	90.8	234.8	371.1
Denmark		9.5	47.4	75.6
France	134.1	439.5	669.3	793.0
Germany	135.0	241.0	688.5	1,097.5
Holland	20.0	97.2	251.1	680.0
Italy		111.2(1862)	213.0	258.3
Norway		18.3(1866)	28.4	43.6
Sweden	8.0	23.2	63.4	104.9
Switzerland		84.0	108.0	160.1
Other Europe				
Bulgaria	--	--	7.4	10.4
Finland	1.9(1841)	4.4	23.8	38.2
Greece	--	4.6	11.6	19.8
Portugal	8.5	17.5	26.6	33.4
Roumania	5.4	13.5	42.3	54.0
Russia	67.0	132.4	247.9	369.0
Servia	--	2.8	6.8	12.8
Spain	16.5	51.3	123.0	115.2
Turkey	--	45.0	40.0	71.5
Northern America				
Canada	15.6	36.2	68.9	148.0
Newfoundland	4.4	6.2	5.7	8.6
United States	111.7	316.2	823.9	1,370.8
Central America				
Central American Republics:			14.3	
Costa Rica	--	1.5	2.1(1883)	6.2
Guatemala	--	1.9	--	7.5
Honduras	--	.3	--	5.9
Nicaragua	--	.3	--	2.8
San Salvador		2.3	--	3.7
Cuba	23.4 (1842)		--	45.2
Haiti				13.3
Mexico		--	29.7	74.6
Puerto Rico	5.1	5.5	--	6.6
San Domingo	--	--	15.0	6.0
West Indies:				
British	25.9	20.4	27.2	24.7
French	7.4	8.6	12.6	8.2

Table A-3 (contd.)

	1840	1860	1880	1900
South America				
Argentina	7.0(1842)	13.8(1861)	56.3	149.2
Bolivia	-	-	-	16.0
Brazil	27.7	57.4	96.2	195.0(1901
Chile	7.0	25.5	51.6	60.7
Colombia	1.2	11.8	22.4	10.5
Ecuador	.9	2.1	3.7	7.7
Guianas:				
British	8.2	7.4	12.7	10.0
Dutch	-	1.8	1.4	2.2
French	-	-	1.0(1882)	1.3
Paraguay	-	1.2	-	2.1
Peru	1.9	24.9(1865)	20.0	21.9
Uruguay	-	9.1(1862)	20.4	30.4
Venezuela	4.8	6.9	11.0(1877)	7.7(1903
Africa				
Algeria	.8(1842)	9.5	34.8	44.3
Angola		2.3	4.3
Barbary States	1.5	-	8.9	10.2
Basutoland				.7
British West Africa:				
Gambia	-	-	-	1.0
Gold Coast	-	-	2.4	4.3
Lagos	-	-	2.8	3.7
Nigeria	-	-	-	5.6
Sierra Leone	-	1.5	1.8	1.5
Canary Islands			2.9	2.0
Cape of Good Hope	5.4	10.0	37.1	36.6
Egypt	5.3	13.2(1859)	68.7	82.9
French West Africa				
Dahomey				2.4
Guinea				1.9
Ivory Coast				1.6
Kongo				1.5
Senegal		2.6	3.8	6.6
German East Africa				1.1
Kongo Free State	-	-	-	10.1
Madagascar			1.3	2.1
Mauritius	4.6	11.2	18.2	10.3
Reunion		8.9	4.8	3.6
Zanzibar	-	-	2.5	6.0

Table A-3 (contd.)

	1840	1860	1880	1900
Asia				
Aden		.9	6.5	9.8
Borneo				1.6
British India	56.5	136.1	325.0	353.9
Ceylon	2.0	10.9	20.6	29.9
China	37.7(1845)	78.0(1864)	106.2	117.5
Dutch East Indies	30.5	37.0(1859)	68.7	103.7
French Indochina			9.7	30.0
Japan		3.8	25.4	101.8
Korea				4.7
Labuan				1.0
Muscat			1.5	
Persia	1.8	–		9.8
Philippines	4.5(1841)	9.7(1856)	21.1	23.0
Sarawak				4.4
Siam	.	6.5(1864)	8.7	15.2
Straits Settlements	8.0	32.0	63.0	116.4
Oceania				
Australia	7.0	76.4	113.0	153.2
New Zealand	–	2.8	24.4	57.2
Misc.				
Fiji				3.0
Hawaii			4.4	22.6

NOTE: Figures refer to special exports where possible. Also, exports are
       of merchandise   when possible to separate these from flows of
       precious metals. In a few cases, (e.g., Mexico, British Guiana) gold
       and silver were commodity exports and are therefore included in the
       totals.

       Dutch figures are highly questionable, but, following Yates, they are
       included here. San Domingo includes Haiti in 1880.

       In this table and others, blanks typically mean data are not available,
       but, in context, will sometimes imply zero or negligible values.

Source: Table A-4

Table A-4

Sources for Table A-3

	1840	1860	1880	1900
United Kingdom	USSAFC	USSAFC	USSAFC	USSAFC

Other Western Europe

Austria-Hungary	MUL	USSAFC	USSAFC	USSAFC
Belgium	USSAFC	USSAFC	USSAFC	USSAFC
Denmark		SY	USSAFC	USSAFC
France	USSAFC	USSAFC	USSAFC	USSAFC
Germany	MUL	SY	USSAFC	USSAFC
Holland	STRTFC	USSAFC	USSAFC	USSAFC
Italy		USSAFC	USSAFC	USSAFC
Norway		USSAFC	USSAFC	USSAFC
Sweden	MUL	USSAFC	USSAFC	USSAFC
Switzerland		MUL	CRFC	USSAFC

Other Europe

Bulgaria			USSAFC	USSAFC
Finland	USSAFC	USSAFC	USSAFC	USSAFC
Greece		USSAFC	USSAFC	USSAFC
Portugal	M-CS	STRTFC	USSAFC	USSAFC
Roumania	STRTFC	SY	USSAFC	USSAFC
Russia	M-CS	USSAFC	USSAFC	USSAFC
Servia		SY	USSAFC	USSAFC
Spain	STRTFC	USSAFC	USSAFC	USSAFC
Turkey		MUL	MUL	WEBB

Northern America

Canada	STRTC	STRTC	USSAFC	USSAFC
Newfoundland	STRTC	USSAFC	USSAFC	USSAFC
United States	USSAFC	USSAFC	USSAFC	USSAFC

Table A-4 (contd.)

	1840	1860	1880	1900
Central America				
Central American Republics:			CRFC	
Costa Rica		STRTFC	USSAFC	USSAFC
Guatemala		STRTFC		SUND
Honduras		STRTFC		CRFC
Nicaragua		STRTFC		USSAFC
San Salvador		STRTFC		CRFC
Cuba	STRTC			USSAFC
Haiti			CRFC	CRFC
Mexico	M-CS		USSAFC	USSAFC
Puerto Rico	M-CS	SY		CRFC
San Domingo			CRFC	CRFC
West Indies:				
British	STRTFC	USSAFC	USSAFC	USSAFC
French	M-CS	USSAFC	USSAFC	USSAFC
South America				
Argentina	MUL	USSAFC	USSAFC	USSAFC
Bolivia				USSAFC
Brazil	USSAFC	USSAFC	USSAFC	USSAFC
Chile	MUL	USSAFC	USSAFC	USSAFC
Colombia	M-CS	McGreevey	McGreevey	McGreevey
Ecuador	M-CS	STRTFC	CRFC	SUND
Guianas:				
British	Adamson	USSAFC	USSAFC	USSAFC
Dutch		USSAFC	USSAFC	USSAFC
French			USSAFC	USSAFC
Paraguay		STRTFC	–	SUND
Peru	M-CS	SY	CRFC	USSAFC
Uruguay		USSAFC	USSAFC	USSAFC
Venezuela	USSAFC	USSAFC	USSAFC	USSAFC
Africa				
Algeria	STRTFC	STRTFC	USSAFC	USSAFC
Angola			CRFC	CRFC
Barbary States	STRTFC		CRFC	USSAFC
Basutoland				CRFC
British West Africa:				
Gambia			CRFC	
Gold Coast			STRTC	STRTC
Lagos			STRTC	STRTC
Nigeria				STRTC
Sierra Leone		STRTC	STRTC	STRTC

Table A-4 (contd.)

	1840	1860	1880	1900
Africa (contd.)				
Canary Islands			CRFC	CRFC
Cape of Good Hope	STRTC	STRTC	USSAFC	USSAFC
Egypt	STRTFC	STRTFC	USSAFC	USSAFC
French West Africa:				
Dahomey				CRFC
Guinea				CRFC
Ivory Coast				CRFC
Kongo				CRFC
Senegal		STRTFC	CRFC	CRFC
German East Africa		.		CRFC
Kongo Free State				CRFC
Madagascar			USSAFC	USSAFC
Mauritius	STRTC	STRTC	STRTC	USSAFC
Reunion		STRTFC	CRFC	CRFC
Zanzibar			CRFC	STRTC
Asia				
Aden		STRTFC	CRFC	CRFC
Borneo				CRFC
British India	SABI	USSAFC	STRTC	USSAFC
Ceylon	STRTC	USSAFC	USSAFC	USSAFC
China	M-CS	USSAFC	USSAFC	USSAFC
Dutch East Indies	STRTFC	STRTFC	USSAFC	USSAFC
French Indochina			USSAFC	USSAFC
Japan		STRTFC	USSAFC	USSAFC
Korea	–	–	–	USSAFC
Labuan				CRFC
Muscat	–	–	CRFC	–
Persia	STRTFC	–	–	SUND
Philippines	USSAFC	USSAFC	USSAFC	USSAFC
Sarawak	–	–	–	STRTC
Siam		STRTFC	USSAFC	USSAFC
Straits Settlements	M-CS	USSAFC	USSAFC	USSAFC
Oceania				
Australia	STRTC	STRTC	STRTC	STRTC
New Zealand	–	USSAFC	USSAFC	USSAFC
Misc.				
Fiji				CRFC
Hawaii			CRFC	CRFC

Reference Tables for Chapter 3

The data in these tables conform closely but not exactly to the data in Table A–3, in part because different sources were sometimes employed in compiling the commodity data presented here.

Table B-1

Exports of Algeria
1860 - 1901

(millions of dollars)

	1860	1880	1901
Animals	.3	3.0	6.7
Breadstuffs	1.2	10.0	15.5
Esparto grass	–	2.4	1.0
Hides and skins	.7	1.1	2.5
Mineral ores	.5	2.3	1.5
Olive oil	.5	–	.6
Tobacco	1.6	.9	1.4
Wine	–	–	10.3
Wool	1.3	2.6	.9
Other goods	3.4	11.5	10.2
Total	9.5	33.8	50.6

Source: 1860 – STRTFC
         1880 – CRFC
         1901 – USSAFC

Table B-2

Exports of Argentina
1842 - 1900

(millions of dollars)

	1842	1861	1880	1900
Corn	–	–	.3	11.5
Hides and skins	5.0	7.5	16.5	21.5
Linseed	–	–	–	10.3
Meat products				
Beef, frozen	–	–	–	2.4
Beef, jerked	–	–	3.0	1.9
Mutton	–	–	–	4.4
Tallow	.7	–	1.8	2.7
Sugar	–	–	–	1.2
Wheat	–	–	–	46.9
Wood	–	–	–	2.3
Wool	.8	4.2	26.6	27.0
Other goods	.5	2.1	8.1	17.1
Total	7.0	13.8	56.3	149.2

Note: These figures are based on customs valuations which, in the opinion of one 19th century American official, understated the actual values by about one-third.

Source: 1842 - M-CS
         1860 - SY and CRFC
         1880 - CRFC
         1900 - USSAFC.

Table B-3

Exports of Bolivia
1900

(millions of dollars)

	1900
Rubber	4.2
Silver	5.4
Tin	3.4
Other goods	3.0
Total	14.2

Source: SY(1902)

Table B-4

Exports of Brazil
1843 - 1901

(millions of dollars)

	1843	1860	1880	1901
Cocoa	-	.8	-	4.1
Coffee	13.3	30.3	60.0	116.4
Cotton	.7	3.2	3.2	2.2
Hides and skins	1.0	5.0	4.5	6.9
Rubber	-	2.0	6.0	41.9
Sugar	3.0	8.1	15.9	7.5
Tobacco	1.0	4.2	3.1	7.9
Yerba maté	-	-	1.2	4.5
Other goods	4.5	3.8	12.3	4.6
Total	23.5	57.4	96.2	195.0

Source: 1843 - M-CS
         1860 - UKSAFC
         1880 - SY and CRFC
         1901 - USSAFC

Table B-5

Exports of British Guiana
1840 - 1900

(millions of dollars)

	1840	1860	1880	1900
Rum	.9	1.3	.9	1.4
Sugar	5.6	5.4	10.6	5.4
Other goods	1.7	.7	1.2	3.2
Total	8.2	7.4	12.7	10.0

NOTE: About $2 million of 1900 residual is
       of gold, a product which enjoyed a brief
       boom in the 1890s and early 1900s.

Source: 1840 - Adamson (1972, p. 215)
         1860-1900 - STRTC and USSAFC

Table B-6

Exports of British India
1840 - 1900

(millions of dollars)

	1840	1860	1880	1900
Coffee	-	.9	8.0	4.8
Cotton				
Raw	9.6	23.0	55.5	32.2
Mfg.	-	3.8	8.0	26.4
Hides and skins				
Raw	-	2.2	18.5	22.4
Dressed	-	-	-	10.6
Indigo	13.7	10.5	14.5	8.7
Jute				
Raw	-	1.5	22.0	26.2
Mfg.	-	1.7	5.8	20.2
Lac	-	-	1.7	3.7
Opium	6.1	45.0	71.5	26.6
Rice	.4	11.5	41.5	43.5
Seeds	-	7.5	22.5	32.9
Silk	3.7	4.0	2.5	2.3
Spices	-	.5	1.5	1.0
Sugar	4.0	5.0	2.5	1.1
Tea	-	.6	15.2	29.5
Vegetables	-	-	-	1.2
Wheat	3.2	-	5.5	12.7
Wool	-	2.1	5.5	4.4
Other goods	15.8	16.3	22.8	43.5
Total	56.5	136.1	325.0	353.9

Source: 1840 - M-CS
           1860 - STRTC
           1880 - TBI
           1900 - USSAFC

Table B-7

Exports of British West Indies
1840 - 1900

(millions of dollars)

	1840	1860	1880	1900
Cocoa	.1	.9	2.6	5.9
Coffee	3.0	1.2	1.9	.7
Sugar	19.0	12.3	12.4	6.4
Other goods	3.8	5.0	10.3	11.7
Total	25.9	20.4	27.2	24.7

NOTE: USSAFC gives a figure of $30 million
        for total exports in 1900, but this appears
        to include re-exports, while my data
        relate to special exports only.

Source: 1840 - 1900 - STRTC

Table B-8

Exports of Cape of Good Hope
1860 - 1900

(millions of dollars)

	1860	1880	1900
Copper	.4	1.5	2.4
Diamonds	-	16.8	16.7
Feathers	.1	4.4	4.3
Gold	-	-	4.0
Skins	.7	1.4	1.2
Wool	7.2	12.1	4.1
Other goods	2.1	.9	3.9
Total	10.5	37.1	36.6

NOTE: 1900 happened to be a low year
        for gold exports. In 1899, these
        amounted to about $67 million.

Source: 1860 - UKSAC
          1880 - UKSAC
          1900 - USSAFC

Table B-9

Exports of Ceylon
1840 - 1900

(millions of dollars)

	1840	1860	1880	1900
Coconut oil	.2	.8	1.8	2.2
Coffee	1.1	8.0	14.1	.2
Copra	-	-	-	1.3
Plumbago	-	-	.9	3.2
Tea	-	-	-	17.4
Other goods	.7	2.1	3.8	6.6
Total	2.0	10.9	20.6	29.9

NOTE: The totals include foreign as well as domestic
exports but not bullion and specie.
Source: 1840 - 1880 - UKSAC
1900 - USSAFC

Table B-10

Exports of Chile
1860 - 1900

(millions of dollars)

	1860	1880	1900
Agricultural produce	-	4.3	-
Barley	.4	-	-
Coal and coke	-	-	1.4
Copper	16.1	12.7	7.8
Flour	1.2	-	-
Hides and skins	1.0	-	-
Nitrate of soda	-	14.1	40.1
Silver	.9	3.0	-
Wheat	1.1	5.7	-
Other goods	1.2	11.8	11.4
Total	25.5	51.6	60.7

Source: 1860 - STRTFC
1880 - CRFC
1900 - USSAFC

Table B-11

Exports of China
1845 - 1900

(millions of dollars)

	1845	1864	1880	1900
Braid	-	-	1.7	3.2
Chemicals	-	-	.3	3.0
Clothing	-	-	.4	1.5
Cotton	-	1.1	.2	7.3
Earthenware	-	-	.6	1.2
Firecrackers	-	-	.3	1.2
Hides	-	-	.3	3.1
Matting	-	-	.7	1.7
Paper	-	-	.7	1.9
Provisions	-	-	-	2.0
Silk:				
Raw	6.2	35.8	31.7	27.0
Mfg.	1.9	3.5	7.6	6.2
Other	-	-	2.4	3.3
Skins	-	-	-	1.8
Sugar	-	-	4.5	2.2
Tea	25.7	25.8	50.0	18.8
Tobacco	-	-	-	1.4
Vegetables	-	-	-	4.0
Other goods	3.9	11.8	13.8	25.7
Total	37.7	78.0	106.2	117.5

Source: 1845 - M-CS
1864 - STRTFC
1880 - UKSAFC
1900 - USSAFC

Table B-12

Exports of Costa Rica
1860 and 1900

(millions of dollars)

	1860	1900
Coffee	1.1	3.4
Bananas	-	2.1
Other goods	.4	.7
Total	1.5	6.2

Sources: 1860 - STRTFC
1900 - CRFC

Table B-13

Exports of Cuba
1842 and 1900

(millions of dollars)

	1842	1900
Coffee	3.0	-
Copper	5.0	-
Sugar	11.4	18.1
Tobacco		
Leaf	-	9.7
Cigars	-	11.6
Other goods	4.0	4.8
Total	23.4	45.2

Source: 1842 - M-CS
1900 - USSAFC

Table B-14

Exports of the Dutch East Indies
1840 - 1900

(millions of dollars)

	1840	1859	1880	1900
Chemicals	-	-	-	4.6
Coffee	14.8	12.2	24.0	9.9
Copra	-	-	-	4.1
Hides	-	-	-	1.4
Indigo	2.5	1.4	-	1.0
Petroleum	-	-	-	1.8
Rice	1.2	3.0	-	1.6
Rubber	-	-	-	6.3*
Spices	-	-	-	2.8
Sugar	5.6	13.6	19.2	29.6
Tea	-	-	-	1.7
Tin	-	2.9	3.8	3.1
Tobacco	.5	.6	6.5	12.9
Other goods	5.9	3.3	15.2	22.9
Total	30.5	37.0	68.7	103.7

*5.2 is gutta-percha

NOTE: 1880 and 1900 totals refer to merchandise exports but
include bullion.
Source: 1840 - M-CS
1859 - STRTFC
1880 - Furnivall (1939, p. 207) and USSAFC
1900 - USSAFC

Table B-15

Exports of Ecuador
1900

(millions of dollars)

	1900
Cocoa	5.3
Coffee	.4
Rubber	.5
Other goods	1.5
Total	7.7

Source: CRFC

Table B-16

Exports of Egypt
1840 - 1900

(millions of dollars)

	1840	1859	1880	1900
Cotton				
Raw	.9	5.5	37.3	64.5
Seed	-	.2	7.7	9.7
Rice	.4	.6	1.0	-
Sugar	-	.1	3.2	2.7
Wheat	1.3	1.9	5.3	-
Other goods	3.7	4.9	14.9	6.0
Total	5.3	13.2	69.4	82.9

Source: 1840 - M-CS
         1859 - STRTFC
         1880 - UKSAFC
         1900 - USSAFC

Table B-17

Exports of French Indochina
1900

(millions of dollars)

	1900
Coal	.7
Fish	1.3
Pepper	.7
Rice	20.0
Other goods	7.3
Total	30.0

Source: Trade and Shipping
         of South East Asia,
         Great Britain Board
         of Trade, 1901

Table B-18

Exports of French West Indies
1840 - 1900

(millions of dollars)

	1840	1860	1880	1900
Rum	.4	.4	1.9	1.7
Sugar	6.6	7.2	8.4	5.0
Other goods	.4	1.0	2.3	1.5
Total	7.4	8.6	12.6	8.2

Source: 1840 - M-CS
         1860 - STRTFC
         1880, 1900 - CRFC

Table B-19

Exports of Guatemala
1900

(millions of dollars)

	1900
Coffee	6.5
Other goods	1.0
Total	7.5

Source: CRFC

Table B-20

Exports of Japan
1861 - 1900

(millions of dollars)

	1861	1880	1900
Coal	-	.5	10.0
Copper	-	.4	6.3
Cotton manufactures	-	-	13.2
Earthenware	-	.5	1.3
Fibers	-	-	2.0
Matches	-	.4	2.9
Matting	-	-	1.6
Silk			
Raw	2.6	8.6	22.2
Mfg.	-	.6	12.0
Other	-	.7	1.6
Tea	.6	7.5	4.5
Other goods	.6	6.2	24.2
Total	3.8	25.4	101.8

Source: 1860 - STRTFC
          1880 - Japan in the Beginning of
                 the 20th Century
          1900 - USSAFC

Table B-21

Exports of Mauritius
1840 - 1900

(millions of dollars)

	1840	1860	1880	1900
Sugar	4.2	10.5	15.0	9.4
Other goods	.4	.7	3.2	.9
Total	4.6	11.2	18.2	10.3

Source: 1840 - STRTC
          1860 - UKSAC
          1880 - UKSAC
          1900 - USSAFC

Table B-22

Table B-23

Exports of Mexico
1900

(millions of dollars)

Exports of Peru
1840 - 1902

(millions of dollars)

	1900
Coffee	5.1
Copper	4.7
Hennequen	12.3
Hides and skins	1.7
Lead	1.6
Silver	30.0
Wood	2.7
Other goods	16.5
Total	74.6

	1840	1865	1880	1902
Cotton	.4	3.0	.7	1.5
Guano	.5	12.2	5.0	-
Gums	-	-	-	1.8
Minerals*	-	-	4.1	4.3
Saltpeter	.3	4.0	-	-
Sugar	-	-	5.0	6.0
Wool	.7	2.1	.7	1.1
Other goods	-	3.6	4.5	3.3
Total**	1.9	24.9	20.0	18.0**

Source: USSAFC

*Much of this is probably saltpeter for which no independent data were available after 1860.

**About $2 million of 1902 total represents re-exports, which are probably reflected in the other goods category.

Source: 1840 - M-CS
          1865 - STRTFC
          1880 - est. based on CRFC
          1902 - USSAFC

Table B-24

Exports of the Philippines
1842 - 1900

(millions of dollars)

	1842	1864	1900
Coffee	.1	.6	-
Copra	-	-	1.7
Hemp	-	2.5	11.4
Sugar	1.0	3.9	2.9
Tobacco	-	1.4	2.0
Other goods	3.2	1.8	1.8
Total	4.3	10.2	19.8

NOTE: 1900 figures relate to fiscal year ending June 30

Source: 1842 - M-CS
          1864 - STRTFC and SY
          1900 - USSAFC

Table B-25

Table B-26

Exports of Reunion
1860 - 1900

(millions of dollars)

Exports of San Salvador
1860 and 1900

(millions of dollars)

	1860	1900
Sugar	8.0	2.0
Other goods	.9	1.6
Total	8.9	3.6

	1860	1900
Indigo	1.9	.3
Coffee	–	3.0
Other goods	.4	.4
Total	2.3	3.7

Source: 1860 - STRTFC
         1900 - CRFC

Source: 1860 - STRTFC
         1900 - CRFC

Table B-27

Exports of Senegal
1880 - 1900

(millions of dollars)

	1860	1880	1900
Gums	.8	1.0	.5
Nuts	.8	2.5	4.7
Rubber	–	–	.4
Other goods	1.0	.3	1.0
Total	2.6	3.8	6.6

Source: 1860 - STRTFC
         1880 - CRFC
         1900 - CRFC

Table B-28

Exports of Siam
1864 - 1900

(millions of Dollars)

	1864	1880	1900
Rice	4.5	7.0	10.8
Teak	-	-	1.1
Other goods	2.0	1.7	3.3
Total	6.5	8.7	15.2

NOTE: Port of Bangkok

Source: 1864 - STRTFC
          1880 - est. based on SY and Cheng (1968)
          1900 - USSAFC

Table B-29

Exports of Straits Settlements
1880 - 1900

(millions of dollars)

	1880	1900
Breadstuffs	2.3	3.3
Chemicals	3.6	3.9
Copra	.5	2.2
Cotton goods	7.3	6.0
Fish	1.2	3.2
Fruits and nuts	.6	1.8
Hides	.9	1.3
Opium	6.2	6.0
Pepper	3.2	4.7
Rice	5.8	10.8
Rubber	2.0	.8
Sugar	2.1	2.2
Tin	7.0	29.6
Other goods	20.3	39.6
Total	63.0	116.4

NOTE: 1900 figures does not include exports of
       precious metals
Source: 1880 - CRFC
          1900 - USSAFC

Table B-30

Exports of Uruguay
1861 - 1900

(millions of dollars)

	1861	1879	1900
Breadstuffs	-	.7	1.6
Hides and skins	4.0	5.6	8.3
Meat products			
Beef extract	-	.5	1.4
Beef, Jerked	1.2	2.3	6.2
Tallow	.4	1.2	1.9
Wool	.9	3.6	8.3
Other goods	1.7	2.7	2.7
Total	8.2	16.6	30.4

Source: 1861 - STRTFC
         1879 - CRFC
         1900 - USSAFC

Table B-31

Table of Sources of Exports of Developed Countries

	1840	1860	1880	1900
Austria-Hungary	M-CS	STRTFC	UKSAFC	USSAFC
Belgium	STRTFC	STRTFC	UKSAFC	USSAFC
Denmark	-	-	-	-
France	STRTFC	STRFTC	UKSAFC	USSAFC
Italy	-	STRFTC	UKSAFC	USSAFC
Norway	-	-	UKSAFC	USSAFC
Sweden	-	-	-	USSAFC
United Kingdom	TUKFC	TUKFC	SAUK	USSAFC
Canada	STRTC	STRTC	STRTC	USSAFC
United States	EXDF	EXDF	EXDF	USSAFC

APPENDIX C

Reference Tables for Chapter 4

Totals across receiving regions in this appendix will equal total exports as given in Appendix A only in exceptional cases. Reasons include: (*a*) use of different sources; (*b*) inclusion of precious metals in geographic flows and not in others; (*c*) occasional use of different years because of data limitations; and (*d*) internal inconsistencies within a given source. Nonetheless, the degree of consistency is reasonably high.

Table C-1

Geographic Distribution of Exports of Asia, 1840

(millions of dollars)

	United Kingdom	Other Western Europe	Northern America	Asia	Other
British India	29.9	3.3	1.6	15.4	1.9
Ceylon	1.5			.5	
China (1845)*	26.1		6.4		
Dutch East Indies	1.0	23.0		4.9	.3
Philippines (1842)	1.0		.9	1.1	1.6
Straits Settlements	1.6	.3		5.4	.2

*Estimate based on M-CS

Source: Table C-14

159

Table C-2

Geographic Distribution of Exports of Asia, 1860

(millions of dollars)

	United Kingdom	Other Western Europe	Northern America	Asia	Other
British India	56.3	5.4	5.1	64.1	4.5
Ceylon	8.1	.8	.2	3.2	
China (1864)*	82.5		7.5	.6	
Dutch East Indies (1859)	.3	34.1	.3	1.7	
Straits Settlements (1868)	6.2	.6	1.9	24.2	

*Figure for China probably includes Hong Kong.

NOTE: Straits Settlements is included in these tables because (1) it is not a pure entrepôt as is Hong Kong and (2) much trade from Southeast Asia and the Malayan Peninsula that is not otherwise accounted for is probably caught in Straits Settlements statistics.

Source: Table C-14

Table C-3

Geographic Distribution of Exports of Asia, 1880

(millions of dollars)

	United Kingdom	Other Western Europe	Northern America	Asia	South Africa	North Africa	Other
British India	135.0	46.8	16.5	107.2	6.7	4.5	4.5
Ceylon	14.4	2.0	.8	2.8			.4
China*	39.0	15.5	11.8	12.2			5.9
Dutch East Indies	10.0	34.7	6.7	1.7			2.8
Japan	3.1	8.1	10.9	4.9			
Philippines (1879)	5.2		4.9				7.1
Straits Settlements	10.7	2.9	5.5	39.8			1.1

*About $20 million impossible to allocate because assigned to Hong Kong to be transhipped. According to Mulhall, about two-thirds of Hong Kong's exports were shipped to Britain. Including the omitted data using this assumption changes the text results for 1880 and 1900 (see next table) hardly at all. Also, exports to Hong Kong from other Asian LDCs (e.g. Ceylon) are counted as part of intra-Asian trade since they would not have been reassigned to Europe because of the distance involved.

Source: Table C-14

Table C-4

Geographic Distribution of Exports of Asia, 1900

(millions of dollars)

	United Kingdom	Other Western Europe	Northern America	Asia	South Africa	North Africa	Other
British India	100.2	72.8	25.0	106.1	9.1	17.4	12.4
Ceylon	19.8	3.0	4.6	2.9			2.2
China*	6.9	18.5	10.9	32.3			
Dutch East Indies	1.7	37.3	11.2	36.4			2.8
Japan	5.1	15.1	27.6	45.8			1.6
Philippines	8.1	3.0	3.0	6.1			2.2
Straits Settlements	29.4	9.8	13.2	69.5			

*47 million dollars impossible to allocate. See Table C-3

Source: Table C-14

Table C-5

Geographic Distribution of Exports of South America, 1840

(millions of dollars)

	United Kingdom	Other Western Europe	Northern America	Other
Brazil (1843)	6.5	10.8	5.3	.3
British Guiana	8.0	-	-	
Peru	1.5			
Venezuela	1.0	2.0	.2	1.0

Source: Table C-14

Table C-6

Geographic Distribution of Exports of South America, 1860

(millions of dollars)

	United Kingdom	Other Western Europe	Northern America	South America	Other
Argentina (1862)	2.3	7.6	2.8		.2
Brazil	22.5	12.4	17.3	3.6	3.9
British Guiana	6.7		.5		.1
Chile	14.4	3.0	2.9	4.6	
Dutch Guiana		.7	.4		
Peru (1865)	20.1		2.2		
Uruguay (1861)	1.9	2.5	.5		1.1
Venezuela (1864)	.3	3.4	1.9		1.3

Source: Table C-14

Table C-7

Geographic Distribution of Exports of South America, 1880

(millions of dollars)

	United Kingdom	Other Western Europe	Northern America	South America	Other
Argentina	5.3	35.1	5.1	8.3	2.7
Brazil	25.6	33.8	48.4		2.5
British Guiana	8.4		3.0		.9
Chile	40.1	4.1	2.5	3.6	
Colombia	4.1	5.6	6.0		
Ecuador	3.2				
Peru	12.9	3.8	.8		
Uruguay	4.3	6.1	2.8	4.8	
Venezuela (1877)	.6	7.4	4.5	.3	.4

NOTE: Figure for Chile in column 1 is inconsistent with British import data. True picture for 1880 probably between one in this table and that for 1903 in Table C-8. In general, Chilean trade data, especially that dealing with destinations, are unreliable, in part because of the listing of large quantities of exports "for orders". In practice, this often meant delivering the goods to English ports on the English channel for immediate re-export to the Continent

Source: Table C-14

Table C-8

Geographic Distribution of Exports of South America, 1900

(millions of dollars)

	United Kingdom	Other Western Europe	Northern America	South America	Other
Argentina	23.1	63.1	6.6	10.1	43.4
Brazil (1901)	25.5	74.7	84.8	6.9	3.9
British Guiana	4.6		4.4		.5
Chile (1903)	23.0	33.0	12.0	2.1	1.0
Colombia	1.4	6.8	3.1		
Dutch Guiana	.1	.8	1.2		
Ecuador	1.2	5.2	1.7		
Peru	10.2	3.1	4.6	3.2	
Uruguay	2.0	14.1	1.7	10.8	1.3
Venezuela	.1	4.3	2.7		.5

Source: Table C-14

Table C-9

Geographic Distribution of Exports of Northern Africa, 1840–1900

(millions of dollars)

	United Kingdom	Other Western Europe	Other Europe	Northern America	Other
1840					
Algeria (1842)		.8	.8		
Barbary States (1839)	1.9		.2		
Egypt	.9	2.1	1.6		.7
1860					
Algeria	7.3	8.2			
Egypt (1859)		3.1	1.8		
1880					
Algeria	5.6	24.2	.9	.5	2.2
Barbary States	3.8	3.2	.2		
Egypt	45.4	9.9	12.5	.5	
1900					
Algeria	2.4	38.1	1.0	.3	1.8
Barbary States	1.4	6.6		.6	1.1
Egypt	45.2	21.2	9.3	5.1	1.6

Source: Table C-14

Table C-10.

Geographic Distribution of Exports of Southern Africa, 1840

(millions of dollars)

	United Kingdom	Other
Cape of Good Hope	4.5	.3
Mauritius	4.0	.1
Sierra Leone	.6	.2

Source: Table C-14

Table C-11.

Geographic Distribution of Exports of Southern Africa, 1860

(millions of dollars)

	United Kingdom	Other Western Europe	Other
Cape of Good Hope	6.5	.9	2.6
Mauritius	7.2	1.1	2.3**
Reunion		8.4	.1
Senegal		2.0	
Other*	1.0	.7	.7

* Gambia, Gold Coast, Natal, Sierra Leone
** 1.5 to Australia

Source: Table C-14

Table C-12

Geographic Distribution of Exports of Southern Africa, 1880

(millions of dollars)

	United Kingdom	Other Western Europe	Oceania	Other
Angola	.9			.7
Cape of Good Hope	29.8	.1		1.0
Lagos	3.0	1.3		
Mauritius	2.2	.7	6.0	8.6*
Natal	3.2			
Reunion		3.4		
Senegal		3.8		
Sierra Leone	.5	.7		.4
Other		.3		

*6.0 to British India

Source: Table C-14

Table C-13

Geographic Distribution of Exports of Southern Africa, 1900

(millions of dollars)

	United Kingdom	Other Western Europe	Other Europe	Other
Angola			4.0	
Cape of Good Hope	33.4	.1		.3
Dahomey		2.3		
Gambia		1.0		
German West Africa		1.1		
Gold Coast	2.5	1.4		
Kongo Free State		9.6		
Lagos	1.3	2.2		
Madagascar	1.7			
Mauritius	.9	.1		9.0*
Nigeria	3.3	2.3		
Reunion		3.6		
Senegal		5.4		1.2
Other	.9	1.0		4.7

*5.7 to British India

Source: Table C-14

Table C-14

Sources for Reference Tables in Appendix C

	1840	1860	1880	1900
Asia				
British India	M-CS	SABI	TBI	USSAFC
Ceylon	STRTC	STRTC	UKSAC	USSAFC
China	M-CS	STRTFC	UKSAFC	USSAFC
Dutch East Indies	STRTFC	STRTFC	CRFC	USSAFC
Japan	–	–	CRFC	USSAFC
Philippines	M-CS	–	CRFC	USSAFC
Straits Settlements	M-CS	STRTC	UKSAC	USSAFC

Table C-14

(contd.)

	1840	1860	1880	1900
South America				
Argentina	M-CS	CRFC	UKSAFC	USSAFC
Brazil	STRTFC	STRTFC	CRFC	USSAFC
British Guiana	Adamson (1972)	STRTC	STRTC	USSAFC
Chile		STRTFC	UKSAFC	SY
Colombia			CRFC	CRFC
Dutch Guiana		STRTFC		CRFC
Ecuador			SY	CRFC
Peru	M-CS	SY	CRFC	USSAFC
Uruguay		STRTFC	CRFC	USSAFC
Venezuela	STRTFC	CRFC	CRFC	USSAFC
Africa				
Algeria	STRTFC	STRTFC	CRFC	USSAFC
Angola			CRFC	CRFC
Barbary States	M-CS	–	CRFC	CRFC
British West Africa:				
Gambia				STRTC
Gold Coast		STRTC	UKSAC	STRTC
Lagos		STRTC	UKSAC	STRTC
Nigeria				STRTC
Sierra Leone	STRTC	STRTC	STRTC	
Canary Islands				
Cape of Good Hope	STRTC	STRTC	STRTC	USSAFC
Egypt	M-CS	STRTFC	UKSAFC	USSAFC
French West Africa:				
Dahomey				CRFC
Senegal	–	STRTFC	CRFC	CRFC
German West Africa				CRFC
Kongo Free State				SY
Madagascar				CRFC
Mauritius	STRTC	UKSAC	UKSAC	USSAFC
Natal			STRTC	STRTC
Reunion	–	STRTFC	CRFC	SY

APPENDIX **D**

World Trade in Selected Goods, 1840–1900

This appendix presents data that can be used to estimate the value of world trade in some products for certain years. It must be emphasized, however, that the totals would typically underestimate the actual value of trade in a given good in a given year because of the frequent unavailability of product-by-product breakdowns. The case of Chilean copper in 1840 illustrates the point, as does the omission of Cuba as a sugar exporter in 1860 and 1880. Users of the data will want to allow for this problem in their own ways.

Table D-1

Value of Exports of Raw Cotton,
Selected Countries, 1840 – 1900

(millions of dollars)

	1840	1860	1880	1900
Brazil	.7	3.2	3.2	2.2
China	–	1.1	.2	7.3
Egypt	.9	5.5	37.3	64.5
British India	9.6	23.0	55.5	32.2
Peru	.4	3.0	.7	1.5
United States	64.9	191.8	211.5	241.9

Source: Appendix B

Table D-2

Value of Exports of Coffee,
Selected Countries, 1840 - 1900

(millions of dollars)

	1840	1860	1880	1900
Brazil	13.3	30.3	60.0	116.4
British India	-	.9	8.0	4.8
British West Indies	3.0	1.2	1.9	.7
Central America:	-	-	6.5	-
Costa Rica	-	1.1	n.a.	3.4
Guatemala	-	-	n.a.	6.5
San Salvador	-	-	n.a.	3.0
Ceylon	1.1	8.0	14.1	.2
Colombia	-	-	-	3.6
Cuba	3.0	-	-	-
Dutch East Indies	14.8	12.2	24.0	9.9
Mexico	-	-	-	5.1

Source: Appendix B. 1900 estimate for Colombia based
on McGreevey (1971).

Table D-3

Value of Exports of Tea,
Selected Countries, 1840 - 1900

(millions of dollars)

	1840	1860	1880	1900
British India	-	.6	15.2	29.5
Ceylon	-	-	-	17.4
China	25.7	25.8	50.0	18.8
Dutch East Indies	-	-	-	1.7
Japan	-	.6	7.5	4.5

Source: Appendix B

Table D-4

Value of Exports of Raw Silk,
Selected Countries, 1840 - 1900

(millions of dollars)

	1840	1860	1880	1900
LDCs				
China	6.2	35.8	31.7	27.0
British India	3.7	4.0	2.5	2.3
DCs				
Austria-Hungary	13.8	7.6	–	–
France	.8	5.2	31.3	19.7
Japan	–	2.6	8.6	22.2
Switzerland	–	–	3.5	3.2

Note: Italy also exported raw silk but exact data
       are unavailable.

Source: Appendix B

Table D-5

Value of Exports of Rubber,
Selected Countries, 1880 - 1900

(millions of dollars)

	1880	1900
Asia		
British India	–	.5
Dutch East Indies	–	5.2
Straits Settlements	2.0	.8
South America		
Brazil	6.0	41.9
Bolivia	–	4.2
Ecuador	–	.5
Africa		
Angola	–	4.1
French Guinea	–	1.5
Gold Coast	–	1.6
Ivory Coast	–	.9
Kongo Free State	–	8.8
Senegal	–	.4
Other Africa	.5	2.7

Source: Asia and South America - Appendix B
         Africa - CRFC

Table D-6

. Value of Exports of Tin,
Selected Countries, 1840 - 1900

(millions of dollars)

	1840	1860	1880	1900
Bolivia	-	-	-	3.4
Dutch East Indies	1.1	2.9	3.8	3.1
Straits Settlements	-	1.4	7.0	29.6

Source: Appendix B. 1860 figure for Straits
Settlements from STRTC.

Table D-7

Value of Exports of Oilseeds,
Selected Countries, 1860 - 1900

(millions of dollars)

	1860	1880	1900
British India	7.5	22.5	32.9
Egypt	.2	7.7	9.7

Source: Appendix B

Table D-8

Value of Exports of Tobacco Leaf,
Selected Countries, 1840 - 1900

(millions of dollars)

	1840	1860	1880	1900
Algeria	-	1.4	.6	.6
Brazil	1.0	4.2	3.1	7.9
China	-	-	-	1.4
Cuba	-	-	-	9.7
Dutch East Indies	.5	.6	6.5	12.9
Egypt	-	-	-	1.8
Philippines	-	1.4	-	.8
United States	9.9	15.9	16.4	29.2

Source: Appendix B

Table D-9

Value of Exports of Nuts,
Selected Countries, 1860 - 1900

(millions of dollars)

	1860	1880	1900
Asia			
Ceylon	.3	.6	.5
Dutch East Indies	-	-	1.1
Straits Settlements	-	.6	1.8
Africa			
Gambia	.4	.5	1.1
Gold Coast	-	.2	.7
Lagos	-	1.7	2.0
Morocco	-	.4	1.6
Senegal	.8	2.5	4.7
Sierra Leone	.3	.6	1.3
Other Africa	-	-	4.5

Source: Asia - Appendix B
          Africa - CRFC and STRTC

Table D-10

Value of Exports of Cocoa,
Selected Countries, 1840 - 1900

(millions of dollars)

	1840	1860	1880	1900
Asia				
Ceylon	-	-	-	.5
South America				
Brazil	-	.8	-	4.1
Dutch Guiana	-	-	-	.9
Ecuador	-	-	-	5.3
Central America				
British West Indies	.1	.9	2.6	5.9
French West Indies	-	.4	.3	.3

Source: Appendix B

Table D-11

Value of Exports of Fertilizer,*
Selected Countries, 1840 - 1900

(millions of dollars)

	1840	1865	1880	1900
British India	-	-	2.3	1.2
Chile	-	-	14.1	40.1
Peru	.8	16.2	9.1	4.3

*guano + nitrate of soda + saltpeter

Source: Appendix B

Table D-12

Value of Exports of Rice,
Selected Countries, 1840 - 1900

(millions of dollars)

	1840	1860	1880	1900
British India	.4	11.5	41.5	43.5
Dutch East Indies	1.2	3.0	-	1.6
Egypt	.4	.6	1.0	-
Indochina	-	-	n.a.	20.0
Italy	-	-	6.4	3.0
Japan	-	-	.2	1.8
Korea	-	-	-	1.8
Siam	-	4.5	7.0	10.8
Straits Settlements	-	.5	5.8	10.8

Source: Appendix B

Table D-13

Value of Exports of Copper,
Selected Countries, 1840 - 1900

(millions of dollars)

	1840	1860	1880	1900
LDCs				
Chile	n.a.	16.1	12.7	7.8
Cuba	5.0	-	-	-
Mexico	-	-	-	4.7
DCs				
Canada	-	-	.7	1.9
Cape of Good Hope	-	.4	1.5	2.4
United Kingdom*	3.7	3.7	5.3	6.8
United States**	-	1.7	3.0	1.2
Other				
Portugal	-	-	1.9	1.2
Spain	-	1.0	11.4	9.8

*Most of this is probably ore from other countries
smelted in the United Kingdom.

**Ore. Most U.S. production used domestically.

Source: Appendix B. Portugal and Spain from UKSAFC
and USSAFC.

Table D-14

Value of Exports of Sugar (Raw and Refined),
Selected Countries, 1840 – 1900

(millions of dollars)

	1840	1860	1880	1900
Europe				
Austria-Hungary	-	-	14.0	37.9
Belgium	-	.1	6.7	15.3
France	-	-	3.0	21.0
Germany	-	-	39.5	51.5
Russia	-	-	n.a.	13.0
Latin America				
British Guiana	5.6	5.4	10.6	5.4
Brazil	3.0	8.1	15.9	7.5
British West Indies	19.0	12.3	12.4	6.4
Cuba	11.4	n.a.	n.a.	18.1
Danish West Indies	-	-	1.0	2.1
Dutch Guiana	-	1.4	n.a.	.5
French West Indies	6.6	7.2	8.4	5.0
Peru	-	-	5.0	6.0
Asia				
British India	4.0	5.0	2.5	1.1
China	-	-	4.5	2.2
Dutch East Indies	5.6	13.6	19.2	29.6
Philippines	1.0	3.9	n.a.	2.9
Straits Settlements	-	-	2.1	2.2
Africa				
Egypt	-	.1	3.2	2.7
Mauritius	4.2	10.5	15.0	9.4
Reunion	n.a.	8.0	n.a.	2.0

Source: Appendix B

Table D-15

Value of Exports of Hides and Skins,
Selected Countries, 1840 – 1900

(millions of dollars)

	1840	1860	1880	1900
LDCs				
Algeria	-	.7	1.1	2.5
Brazil	1.0	5.0	4.5	6.9
British India	-	2.2	18.5	22.4
China	-	-	.3	3.1
Dutch East Indies	-	-	-	1.0
Straits Settlements	-	-	.9	1.4
DCs				
Argentina	5.0	11.7	16.5	21.5
Australia	-	-	2.0	5.2
Belgium	6.3	7.2	7.4	9.2
Canada	-	-	.7	1.3
Denmark	-	-	-	2.0
France	-	4.3	30.9	21.2
Germany	-	-	20.2	24.6
Italy	-	1.0	1.5	4.2
Netherlands	-	-	4.0	7.6
New Zealand	-	-	-	1.4
Sweden	-	-	-	1.2
United Kingdom	-	-	-	7.1
Other				
Portugal	-	-	.2	-
Roumania	-	1.0	1.0	.5
Russia	1.4	n.a.	n.a.	7.3
Spain	-	.3	1.2	2.0

Sources: Appendix B. Other from UKSAFC and USSAFC

Table D-16

Value of Exports of Wheat,
Selected Countries, 1840 – 1900

(millions of dollars)

	1840	1860	1880	1900
LDCs				
British India	3.2	-	5.5	12.7
Chile	-	1.1	5.7	-
Egypt	1.3	1.9	5.3	-
Uruguay	-	-	-	1.0
DCs				
Argentina	.7	-	-	46.9
Austria-Hungary	.2	.9	10.4	-
Belgium	.2	n.a.	n.a.	7.5
Canada	.4	4.7	5.9	12.0
France	-	10.8	n.a.	3.4
Germany	-	-	-	9.2
Italy	-	5.3	4.8	n.a.
New Zealand	-	-	.4	1.7
United Kingdom	-	-	1.7	0
United States	1.6	4.1	190.6	73.2
Other				
Roumania	2.3	5.0	14.4	19.5
Russia	11.5	28.0	42.5	53.7
Servia	-	-	-	2.2

Source: Appendix B

Table D-17

Value of Exports of Silk Manufactures,
Selected Countries, 1840 – 1900

(millions of dollars)

	1840	1860	1880	1900
LDCs				
British India	2.0	.9	1.0	-
China	1.9	3.5	7.6	6.2
DCs				
France	25.6	100.7	46.9	61.5
Germany	-	-	n.a.	39.6
Italy	n.a.	48.1	56.5	86.6
Japan	-	-	1.3	13.6
Switzerland	n.a.	n.a.	36.8	40.7
United Kingdom	4.0	12.0	13.6	10.0

Source: Appendix B

Table D-18

Value of Exports of Jute Manufactures,
Selected Countries, 1840 - 1900

(millions of dollars)

	1840	1860	1880	1900
British India	–	1.7	5.8	20.2
United Kingdom	–	1.0	12.3	11.5

Source: Appendix B

Table D-19

Value of Exports of Dyes and Dyestuffs,
Selected Countries and Regions, 1840 - 1900

(millions of dollars)

	1840	1860	1880	1900
LDCs				
British Honduras	–	–	.4	.6
British India	13.7	10.5	14.5	8.7
Central American Republics	–	2.1	n.a.	–
Dutch East Indies	2.5	1.4	–	1.0
Haiti and Santo Domingo	n.a.	n.a.	4.0	n.a.
Mexico	–	–	–	.9
Philippines	.3	.1	–	–
Venezuela	.2	–	–	–
DCs				
France	.3	3.6	7.4	4.7
Germany	–	–	22.2	20.8
Italy	–	2.0	1.9	1.5
Netherlands	–	–	5.8	9.1
Switzerland	–	–	–	3.0
United Kingdom	–	–	–	1.6
United States	–	–	.7	.5

Source: Appendix B

Table D-20

Value of Exports of Hemp,
Selected Countries, 1840 - 1900

(millions of dollars)

	1840	1860	1880	1900
LDCs				
British India	-	-	.2	.8
China	-	-	-	.8
Philippines	-	2.5	-	11.4
DCs				
Belgium	-	-	-	3.1
Italy	-	4.0	4.6	8.4
Netherlands	-	-	-	2.9
Other				
Russia	7.5	6.0	8.8	4.2

Source: Appendix B

Table D-21

Value of Exports of Cotton Manufactures,
Selected Countries, 1840 - 1900

(millions of dollars)

	1840	1860	1880	1900
LDCs				
Ceylon	-	.9	.6	-
British India	-	3.8	7.0	26.4
DCs				
Austria-Hungary	-	-	-	4.6
Belgium	1.2	3.5	5.6	8.3
France	14.4	17.1	15.8	34.9
Germany	n.a.	n.a.	29.5	67.1
Italy	-	-	n.a.	11.8
Japan	-	-	-	13.2
Netherlands	n.a.	n.a.	11.1	16.2
Switzerland	n.a.	n.a.	12.9	32.9
United Kingdom	122.5	259.3	377.1	339.8
United States	3.5	10.9	10.0	24.0
Other				
Portugal	-	-	-	2.4
Russia	-	2.7	n.a.	6.0
Spain	-	-	-	5.1

Source: Appendix B

References

Adamson, A. *Sugar Without Slaves*. New Haven, Conn.: Yale University Press, 1972.

Ahmed, R. *The Progress of the Jute Industry and Trade, 1855–1966*. Dacca: Central Jute Committee, 1966.

Allen, N. *The Opium Trade*. Boston: Milford House, 1953.

Allen, R. G. D., and Ely, J. E. *International Trade Statistics*. New York: Wiley, 1953.

Anstey, V. *The Economic Development of India*. London: Longmans, 1939.

Ashworth, W. *A Short History of the International Economy Since 1850*. London: Longmans, 1952.

Bairoch, P. *The Economic Development of the Third World Since 1900*. London: Methuen & Co., 1975.

Bairoch, P. "European Foreign Trade in the XIX Century: The Development of the Value and Volume of Exports." *Journal of European Economic History* 3 (Winter 1974): 557–608.

Bairoch, P. "Free Trade and European Economic Development in the 19th Century." *European Economic Review* 3 (Nov. 1972): 211–245.

Bairoch, P. "Geographical Structure and Trade Balance of European Foreign Trade from 1800 to 1970." *Journal of European Economic History* 3 (1974): 557–608.

Baldwin, R. *Economic Development and Export Growth: A Study of Northern Rhodesia, 1920–1960*. Berkeley: University of California Press, 1966.

Baldwin, R. "Patterns of Development in Newly Settled Regions." *Manchester School of Economic and Social Studies* 24 (May 1956): 161–179.

Barker, P. W. *Rubber Industry of the United States, 1839–1959*. Wasthington D.C.: U.S. Commerce Department, 1939.

Beckford, G. L. *Persistent Poverty*. London: Oxford University Press, 1972.

Bhatia, B. M. "Terms of Trade and Economic Development: A Case Study of India—1861–1939." *Indian Economic Journal* 16 (Apr.–June 1969): 414–433.

Brookfield, H. *Interdependent Development*. London: Methuen & Co., 1975.

Brown, N., and Turnbull, C. *A Century of Copper*. London: Wilson & Co., 1906.

Chambers, E. J., and Gordon, D. F. "Primary Products and Economic Growth: An Empirical Measurement." *Journal of Political Economy* 74 (Aug. 1966): 315–332.

Cheng, S. *The Rice Industry of Burma, 1852–1940*. Singapore: University of Malaya Press, 1968.

Clapham, J. *The Economic Development of France and Germany, 1815–1914.* 4th ed. London: Cambridge University Press, 1968.

Cohen, B. *The Question of Imperialism.* New York: Basic Books, 1973.

Cole, W. A., and Deane, P. *British Economic Growth, 1688–1959.* London: Cambridge University Press, 1962.

Cole, W. A., and Deane, P. "The Growth of National Incomes." In *The Cambridge Economic History of Europe,* vol. 6, edited by H. J. Habbakkuk and M. Postan, pp. 1–59. London: Cambridge University Press, 1966.

Day, C. *A History of Commerce.* New York: Longmans, Green & Co., 1922.

Deane, P. *The First Industrial Revolution.* London: Cambridge University Press, 1965.

Durand, J. "The Modern Expansion of World Population." *Proceedings of the American Philosophical Society* 110 (Nov. 1966): 136–159.

Eisner, G. *Jamaica, 1830–1930: A Study in Economic Growth.* Manchester: Manchester University Press, 1961.

Evans, H. *Exports, Domestic and Foreign, from the United States to All Countries, 1789–1883.* Washington, D.C.: U.S. Government Printing Office, 1884.

Fenichel, A. H., and Huff, W. G. *The Impact of Colonialism on Burmese Economic Development.* McGill University Occasional Paper Series, no. 7. Montreal: McGill University Press, 1971.

Frank, A. G. "Multilateral Trade Imbalances and Uneven Economic Development." *Journal of European Economic History* 5 (1976): 407–408.

Furnivall, J. S. *Netherlands India.* London: Cambridge University Press, 1939.

Gates, W. B. *Michigan Copper and Boston Dollars.* Cambridge, Mass.: Harvard University Press, 1951.

General Agreement on Tariffs and Trade, *International Trade.* Geneva: 1970.

Golob, E. O. *The Meline Tariff: French Agriculture and Nationalist Economic Policy.* New York: AMS Press, 1968.

Good, D. "Stagnation and Take-Off in Austria, 1873–1913." *Economic History Review,* 2d ser. 27 (Feb. 1974): 72–87.

Great Britain, Board of Trade. *Annual Statement of the Trade of the United Kingdom with Foreign Countries.* London (various years).

———. *Statistical Abstract of Colonies.* London (various years).

———. *Statistical Abstract of Foreign Countries.* London (various years).

———. *Statistical Tables Relating to the Colonial and Other Possessions of the United Kingdom.* London (various years). Title varies.

———. *Tables Relating to Foreign Countries.* London (various years).

———. *Trade and Shipping of Southeast Asia.* London (various years).

———. *Statistical Abstract of the United Kingdom.* London (various years).

Great Britain, India Office. *Statistical Abstract of British India.* London (various years).

Greenberg, M. *British Trade and the Opening of China, 1800–42.* Cambridge: Cambridge University Press, 1951.

Hanson, J. R. II. "The Leff Conjecture: Some Contrary Evidence." *Journal of Political Economy* 84 (Apr. 1976): 401–405.

Hanson, J. R. II. "More on Trade as a Handmaiden of Growth." *The Economic Journal* 87 (Sept. 1977): 554–557.

Hanson, J. R. II. "Exchange-Rate Movements and Economic Development in the Late Nineteenth Century: A Critique." *Journal of Political Economy* 83 (Aug. 1975): 859–862.

Hershlag, Z. Y. *Introduction to the Economic History of the Middle East.* Netherlands: E. J. Brill, 1964.

Hilgerdt, F. *Industrialization and Foreign Trade.* Geneva: League of Nations, 1945.

Hill, P. *The Migrant Cocoa Farmers of Southern Ghana: A Study in Rural Capitalism.* Cambridge: Cambridge University Press, 1963.

Hirschman, A. *National Power and the Structure of Foreign Trade.* Berkeley: University of California Press, 1945.

Hobsbawm, E. J. *Industry and Empire.* New York: Pantheon, 1968.

Imlah, A. *Economic Elements in the Pax Brittanica.* Cambridge, Mass.: Harvard University Press, 1958.

Ingram, J. *Economic Change in Thailand Since 1850.* Stanford, Calif.: Stanford University Press, 1955.

Issawi, C. "The Economic Development of Egypt, 1800–1960." In *The Economic History of the Middle East,* edited by Charles Issawi, pp. 369–374. Chicago: University of Chicago Press, 1966.

Japan Department of Agriculture and Commerce. *Japan in the Beginning of the 20th Century.* London: J. Murray, 1904.

Jones, J. H. *The Tinplate Industry.* London: P. S. King & Son, 1914.

Khalaf, N. G. "Country Size and Trade Concentration." *Journal of Development Studies* 2 (Oct. 1974): 81–85.

Kindleberger, C. P. *Foreign Trade and the National Economy.* New Haven, Conn.: Yale University Press, 1962.

Knight, Charles L. *Secular and Cyclical Movements in the Production and Price of Copper.* Philadelphia: University of Pennsylvania Press, 1935.

Kravis, I. "Trade as a Handmaiden of Growth: Similarities between the Nineteenth and Twentieth Centuries." *Economic Journal* 80 (Dec. 1970): 850–872.

Kravis, I. "External Demand and Internal Supply Factors in LDC Export Performance." *Banca Nazionale del Lavoro Quarterly Review* 23 (June 1970): 3–25.

Kravis, I. "The Role of Exports in Nineteenth Century United States Growth." *Economic Development and Cultural Change* 20 (Apr. 1972): 387–405.

Kuznets, S. "The Level and Structure of Foreign Trade: Long-Term Trends." *Economic Development and Cultural Change* 14 (Jan. 1967): 1–140.

Lambi, I. M. *Free Trade and Protection in Germany, 1869–1879.* Weisbaden: Franz Steiner Verlag GMBH, 1963.

Landes, D. *The Unbound Prometheus.* Cambridge, Mass.: Harvard University Press, 1969.

Latham, A. J. H. "Merchandise Trade Imbalances and Uneven Economic Development in India and China." *Journal of European Economic History* 7 (1978): 33–60.

Leff, N. "Tropical Trade and Development in the Nineteenth Century: The Brazilian Experience." *Journal of Political Economy* 81 (May–June 1973): 678–696.

Lewis, W. A. *Aspects of Tropical Trade, 1883–1965.* Stockholm: Almqvist & Wicksell, 1969.

Lewis, W. A. *The Evolution of the International Economic Order.* Princeton, N.J.: Princeton University Press, 1978.

Lewis, W. A. *Growth and Fluctuations, 1870–1913.* London: George Allen & Unwin, 1978.

Lewis, W. A., ed. *Tropical Development, 1880–1913.* Evanston, Ill.: Northwestern University Press, 1970.

Levin, J. *The Export Economies.* Cambridge, Mass.: Harvard University Press, 1960.

Lim, Y. "Trade and Development: The Case of Ceylon." *Economic Development and Cultural Change* 16 (Jan. 1968): 245–260.

Macgregor, J. *Commercial Statistics.* London: Whitaker Publishers, 1847.

Maddison, A. *Class Structure and Economic Growth.* New York: Norton, 1971.

Maddison, A. "Growth and Fluctuation in the World Economy, 1870–1960." *Banca Nazionale del Lavoro Quarterly Review* 15 (June 1962): 127–195.

Magdoff, H. *The Age of Imperialism.* New York: Monthly Review Press, 1969.

Mandle, J. R. *The Plantation Economy.* Philadelphia: Temple University Press, 1974.

Mathias, P. *The First Industrial Nation.* London: Methuen & Co., 1969.

Mauro, F. "Toward an Intercontinental Model: European Overseas Expansion between 1500 and 1800." *Economic History Review.* 2d ser. 14 (1961): 1–17.

McCloskey, D. "The Achievements of the Cliometric School." *Journal of Economic History* 38 (Mar. 1978): 13–28.

McCloskey, D. "Did Victorian Britain Fail?" *Economic History Review.* 2d. ser. 23 (Dec. 1970): 446–459.

McCloskey, D. "Victorian Growth: A Rejoinder." *Economic History Review.* 2d. ser. 27 (May 1974): 275–277.

Morgan, T. *Economic Development.* New York: Harper & Row, 1975.

Morris, M. *The Emergence of an Industrial Labor Force in India: A Study of the Bombay Cotton Mills, 1854–1947,* Berkeley: University of California Press, 1965.

Mukerji, M. "National Income." In *Economic History of India, 1857–1956,* edited by V. Singh, pp. 661–703. Bombay: Allied Publishing Co., 1965.

Mulhall, Michael. *Dictionary of Statistics.* London, George Routledge & Co., 1888.

Myint, H. *Economic Theory and the Underdeveloped Countries.* New York: Oxford University Press, 1971.

Nugent, J. "Exchange-Rate Movements and Economic Development in the Late Nineteenth Century." *Journal of Political Economy* 81 (Sept. 1973): 1110–1135.

Nurkse, R. *Equilibrium and Growth in the World Economy.* Cambridge, Mass.: Harvard University Press, 1961.

Owen, E. R. J. *Cotton and the Egyptian Economy, 1820–1914.* London: Oxford University Press, 1969.

Ponting, K. G. "Logwood: An Interesting Dye." *Journal of European Economic History* 2 (Spring 1973): 109–119.

Sauerbeck, Augustus. "The Prices of Commodities and the Precious Metals." *Journal of the Royal Statistical Society* 48 (Sept. 1886): 581–648.

Saul, S. B. *The Myth of the Great Depression, 1873–1896.* London: Macmillan, 1969.

Schultz, H. *The Theory and Measurement of Demand.* Chicago: University of Chicago Press, 1938.

Schultz, T. W. *Transforming Traditional Agriculture.* New Haven, Conn.: Yale University Press, 1964.

Scott, J. M. *The Tea Story.* London: Heineman Ltd., 1964.

Silver, A. W. *Manchester Men and Indian Cotton.* Manchester: Manchester University Press, 1966.

Simkin, C. G. F. *The Traditional Trade of Asia.* London: Oxford University Press, 1968.

Snodgrass, D. *Ceylon: An Export Economy in Transition.* Homewood, Ill.: Richard D. Irwin, 1966.

Statesman's Yearbook. London: Macmillan & Co. (various years).

Stein, S. *Vassouras.* Cambridge, Mass.: Harvard University Press, 1957.

Sundbärg, G. *Apercus Statistiques Internationaux.* New York: Gordon & Breach Science Publishers, 1908.

Taussig, F. W. *The Tariff History of the United States.* New York: Augustus M. Kelley Publishers, reprinted 1967.

Tollison, R. D., and Willett, T. D. "International Integration and the Interdependence of Economic Variables." *International Organization* 27 (Spring 1974): 255–272.

Tooke, T. *History of Prices.* London: Longmans, 1857.

U.S. Department of Commerce and Labor. *Statistical Abstract of Foreign Countries.* Washington, D.C.: U.S. Government Printing Office, 1909.

_____. *Commercial Relations of the United States with Foreign Countries.* Washington, D.C.: U.S. Government Printing Office.

Webb, A. *Dictionary of Statistics.* London: George Routledge & Sons, 1911.

Williamson, J. G. "Late Nineteenth-Century American Retardation: A Neoclassical Analysis." *Journal of Economic History* 33 (Sept. 1973): 581–607.

Woodruff, W. *The Rise of the British Rubber Industry in the 19th Century.* Liverpool: Liverpool University Press, 1968.

Woodruff, W. *The Impact of Western Man.* New York: St. Martin's Press, 1967.

Wright, G. *The Political Economy of the Cotton South.* New York: W. W. Norton & Co., 1978.

Wright, G. "An Econometric Study of Cotton Production and Trade, 1830–1860." *Review of Economics and Statistics* 53, no. 2 (May 1971): 111–120.

Wright, G. "Cotton Competition and the Post-Bellum Recovery of the American South." *Journal of Economic History* 34 (Sept. 1974): 610–635.

Yales, P. L. *Forty Years of Foreign Trade.* New York: Macmillan & Co., 1969.

Youngson, A. J. "The Opening Up of New Territories." In *The Cambridge Economic History of Europe,* vol. 6, edited by H. J. Habakkuk and M. Postan, pp. 139–211. London: Cambridge University Press, 1966.

Zimmerman, L. F. "The Distribution of World Income, 1860–1960." In *Essays on Unbalanced Growth,* edited by E. De Vries, pp. 39–54. The Hague: Mouton & Co., 1962.

Subject Index

A

Africa, 54, *see also* specific country
  balance of payments in, 125T
  diversification of trade partners of, 91
  economic development of, 131, 132
  exports–national-product ratio of, 23
  exports of, 20, 22, 57–58, 59T, 67
    destination of, 55T, 166T–168T
    growth of, 60
    value of, 140T
  Northern, 11
    exports of, 64T, 65, 166T
  Southern, 11, 17, 28, 41n, 54
    exports of, 41n, 65, 66, 108, 167T–168T
  in world trade network, 30
Agriculture, *see also* Plantations; specific
    product
  in Belgium, 100
  in Brazil, 85
  in Colombia, 86
  in Egypt, 88, 109–110
  in Europe, 100
  and free trade, 117
  in India, 85–86
  in North America, 100
  peasant, 7, 49
  subsistence, 24
  and supply, 84
  tariffs on products of, 100, 112, 116

technological advances in, 75, 84, 88,
    109–110
  in United Kingdom, 74–75, 88, 100, 112,
    130
Alexandria, Egypt, 86
Algeria, 11
  exports of, 65, 145T
  trade restrictions on, by France, 65
Argentina
  exports of, 146T
    surplus of, 128
  modern economic growth in, 11
Asia, 11, 54
  balance of payments in, 125T
  coffee production in, 109
  demand of, for cotton, 98
  diversification of trade partners of, 91
  economic development of, 62, 131, 132
  exports–national-product ratio of, 21, 23,
    24
  exports of, 22, 57, 58, 59T, 61, 62–63, 67,
    104, 106
    destination of, 55T, 60–61, 61T, 62–63,
    159T, 160T, 161T, 162T
    growth of, 60
    share of, in world trade, 17, 20
    value of, 141T
  and intra-Asian trade, 61, 61T, 63, 74, 118
  population growth of, 60n
  rice cultivation in, 86

189